AF898973

Dry Zones

"Elizabeth Jean Taylor's *Dry Zones: Planning and the Hangovers of Liquor Licensing History* is thoroughly researched and well-balanced, and is the most complete description and explanation of the evolution of Melbourne's liquor licensing written to date."

—David Merrett, *University of Melbourne, Australia*

Elizabeth Jean Taylor

Dry Zones

Planning and the Hangovers of Liquor Licensing History

palgrave
macmillan

Elizabeth Jean Taylor
Centre for Urban Research
Royal Melbourne Institute of
Technology (RMIT)
Melbourne, VIC, Australia

ISBN 978-981-13-2786-5 ISBN 978-981-13-2787-2 (eBook)
https://doi.org/10.1007/978-981-13-2787-2

Library of Congress Control Number: 2018956587

© The Editor(s) (if applicable) and The Author(s), under exclusive licence to Springer Nature Singapore Pte Ltd 2019
This work is subject to copyright. All rights are solely and exclusively licensed by the Publisher, whether the whole or part of the material is concerned, specifically the rights of translation, reprinting, reuse of illustrations, recitation, broadcasting, reproduction on microfilms or in any other physical way, and transmission or information storage and retrieval, electronic adaptation, computer software, or by similar or dissimilar methodology now known or hereafter developed.
The use of general descriptive names, registered names, trademarks, service marks, etc. in this publication does not imply, even in the absence of a specific statement, that such names are exempt from the relevant protective laws and regulations and therefore free for general use.
The publisher, the authors and the editors are safe to assume that the advice and information in this book are believed to be true and accurate at the date of publication. Neither the publisher nor the authors or the editors give a warranty, express or implied, with respect to the material contained herein or for any errors or omissions that may have been made. The publisher remains neutral with regard to jurisdictional claims in published maps and institutional affiliations.

Cover illustration: © John Rawsterne/patternhead.com

This Palgrave Pivot imprint is published by the registered company Springer Nature Singapore Pte Ltd.
The registered company address is: 152 Beach Road, #21-01/04 Gateway East, Singapore 189721, Singapore

Acknowledgements

I would like to acknowledge the reviewers of the earlier drafts of this book. Thanks also to Pam Strijder, Judy and Len Taylor, and The Harcourt Heritage Museum especially George Milford for help with local and family history; to Kate Taylor for recordings of our grandmother Una; to Joshua Pitt at Palgrave Macmillan for commissioning the work; and to Robin the cat for sitting at my side (or on my lap/keyboard) while writing. And thanks to the many people who contributed (sometimes inadvertently) ideas and comments on this book's content including: Andrew Bonnici, Scott Boydle, Andrew Butt, Nicole Cook, Kulja Coulston, Graeme Davison, Jennifer Day, Robert Freestone, Brendan Gleeson, Robin Goodman, Annette Kroen, Christian Lamker, Crystal Legacy, Cameron Logan, Clay Lucas, Chris McConville, David Merrett, Luke Miller, David Nichols, Andi Nygaard, Kath Phelan, Helen Rowe, Stephen Rowley, Andrew Taylor, Sarah Taylor (especially for mapping help), Kate Tucker, Ilan Wiesel, Claire Wilkinson, Claire Wright, and to those with whom I have had many productive discussions over a drink at the Clyde Hotel.

Contents

List of Figures

List of Tables

CHAPTER 1

Introduction: Walter's Hotel, 1882

Abstract In this chapter Taylor introduces the influence of local anti-alcohol policies of the temperance movement of the late nineteenth and early twentieth centuries, using an 1882 incident at a hotel in Barkers Creek, central Victoria, as an illustration. Taylor suggests that the closure of all the hotels in Barkers Creek and neighboring Harcourt by the 1920s as a result of local temperance policies and groups reflects a larger story of legal and political change. The chapter introduces "local option" rights and controls of the temperance era, suggesting these smaller prohibitions have been overlooked and warrant re-examination in light of contemporary planning challenges. With international examples but focusing on Victoria, the structure of the "Dry Zones" book is outlined, seeking to offer a new perspective on the rise of democratic controls on alcohol, their influence on liquor licensing and early zoning ideas, and their legacies for cities and planning today.

Keywords Temperance · Prohibition · Urban history
Planning history · Australia

On August 12, 1882, the Castlemaine Police Court report in the *Bendigo Advertiser* recounted how one John Wilkinson had been charged with "unlawfully and maliciously afflicting grievous bodily harm" on a Barkers Creek hotelkeeper, John Walters. The hotelkeeper recalled how:

© The Author(s) 2019

E. J. Taylor, *Dry Zones*, https://doi.org/10.1007/978-981-13-2787-2_1

> The accused came to his hotel on the 29 July, about 11 o'clock p.m., with a man named G. Rutledge, and called for four drinks. Wilkinson asked who was going to pay for them. Sauvarin said, "Well, you asked for them; but if you won't pay for them I will." Wilkinson said, "Oh, b______ it, here you are then," placing two shillings on the counter. Wilkinson then threw the contents of his glass on the ground, and said he would fight any ____ man in the house. ("Police Court", *Bendigo Advertiser*, Saturday August 12, 1882, p. 2)

Some of the words considered at the time to be swear words have been blanked out, possibly to our loss. Wilkinson seems likely to have said "bugger it", and professed to being willing to fight "any bloody man in the house". Even with the guesswork around dated obscenities there is something timelessly familiar about the pub scene and about Wilkinson himself, with his resemblance to other chaotic characters sprinkled through court reports then as now. It is not difficult to still feel the collective sigh in the room as he threw his drink, pointlessly yet pointedly, onto the ground and announced his eagerness to fight someone—anyone, really—phrased as an insistent answer to a question nobody had actually asked. The publican of Walter's Hotel (later renamed the Old England) went on to describe how:

> When he came in he was half drunk. He commenced bouncing about, and I sent my wife out of the bar. Sauvarin and I tried to persuade him to go home peacefully, as he had his little boy in the dray outside.

Although the publican seemed to have persuaded the belligerent Wilkinson to leave, in the end, to cut a long story short, Wilkinson beat him forcefully and nearly lethally over the head with a fence paling. The publican recounted how he had turned to go back inside the hotel when:

> I heard the words, "take that, you ______", and I fell to the ground like a bullock.

Was it "take that, you bugger"? Or worse? In any case, a police constable later described how he had arrested John Wilkinson at his home in nearby White Gum Flat, and that "he was not sober when I arrested him, and did not appear to realise the position he was in". He waited as Wilkinson fumbled with his boots, putting them on the wrong feet. John Wilkinson was later found guilty, and sentenced to two years hard labour.

One hundred and twenty years later, in an interview recorded in 2002, my grandmother Una recalled John "Jack" Wilkinson as "a man who could find gold anywhere", and as someone who was often quickly parted from it at the nearest pub. Wilkinson was my maternal grandmother's grandfather, her father's father, making him a great great grandfather to me. In interviews recorded by my sister Kate, my grandmother (who has since passed away) recalled Wilkinson as a rakishly charming old man, carrying sweets and walking along railway tracks through the bushlands of the old goldfields. A stern, small face stares out from the photograph on his 1882 central prison record (Public Records Office Victoria Series 515, 19481)—he looks almost like a cartoonist's idea of a petty criminal. He existed so long ago that I would hesitate, beyond a slight familiarity of eyebrows and nose ("large", by the official description), to call him a "relation".

Yet there are longer and fainter connections, beyond noses, to Wilkinson and his time. Some survived over a century to be told to me as faintly traced tales illustrative of the dangers of drinking alcohol, and go at least some way to explaining the alcohol-free wine ("Maisons sparkling grape drink") that consistently adorned my family's alcohol-free Christmas tables over a century later. John Wilkinson's wife and children had once, for example, spent the night hiding in reeds at the side of the Harcourt reservoir, as he chased them drunkenly through the darkness with an axe—trying in a sincere if unsuccessful effort to decapitate them all. On another occasion he was said to have attempted to persuade his horse to jump a gate late at night after the pub. When the horse refused, Wilkinson slit its throat. The story has a satisfying note of idiocy: you are left to imagine how he had to open the gate himself, drunken and bloodied, one horse down and no closer to home.

Given his penchant for decapitation, my grandmother summarised what she knew of her grandfather John Wilkinson's character in a relatively understated way. She mentions the experiences of her own father, George—who was, given his birth year in 1885, a younger brother of "the little boy in the dray outside" the hotel in 1882 (likely John Junior). John Wilkinson, she recounted, "wasn't a very nice man when he was younger - when my father was small he used to belt them. And he was drinking. He was just a…". At this point, after a weighty pause, she trails off unenthusiastically in the recording and draws out with surprising finality—"a horrible old man really. He drank". Her decisiveness is surprising to me—in my memory of the moral world of Methodist grandparents, men were divided into "lovely men" and "lovely men, really, except" (except, e.g. when burdened with a horrible wife, or when they drank). Only politicians warranted stronger epitaphs. It is jarring to hear a man described merely as horrible.

It is the "he drank" part that is central to this book. As far as I know, nothing Jack Wilkinson did to his own family (or horse) ever made public record. The hotel fence paling incident was, however, far from his first or his last sketchy appearance in the local press. Intermittent Castlemaine Police Court reports in *The Mount Alexander Mail* suggest a man readily inclined to call upon a repertoire of violence, arson, glass smashing, or at least colourful language in response to perceived obstacles to his obtaining another drink ("The Smash at Morley's Freemasons Hotel", April 24, 1863, "Obscene Language" April 5, 1864, "A Rough Customer", April 25, 1874, "Window Breaking", December 11, 1874, "Assault", April 17, 1878). Yet from these and many similar reports concerning different people it is also clear Wilkinson was not unique, nor were the experiences of his family, nor the hotels he frequented.

Meanwhile at least one of Wilkinson's sons, George Wilkinson, became active in the Methodist Church and a member of temperance group The Independent Order of Rechabites. The district within which the Wilkinsons lived, Harcourt and adjacent Barkers Creek (on the outskirts of Castlemaine—see map at Fig. 1.1), became home to a branch (or "tent") of the Order in 1869. A history of the district notes how "at one time Harcourt was credited with having five hotels but because of the strong influence of the Rechabite Lodge, an organisation with strong anti-alcohol beliefs, these were all closed" (Carr 2002). All twelve of the hotels of both Harcourt and Barkers Creek were, by means both direct and indirect, closed during the course of the late nineteenth and early twentieth centuries. Harcourt earned a "state wide reputation as a temperance district" when, as the last pub was closed and reopened as a Coffee Palace (alcohol free temperance hotel), the pipes were ripped from the cellar to "allow the liquor to run down the gutter" (Houston 2009; also see "A Harcourt Pioneer", *The Bendigonian*, August 25, 1914). For every action, perhaps, there is an equal and opposite reaction.

The story of how and why Harcourt and surrounds came to be without any hotels (or more specifically, without any liquor licenses) is partly about the peculiarities of that district, but more so reflective of a larger story of legal and political change. In this book, I examine how the local level rights and controls around liquor licensing that emerged during the

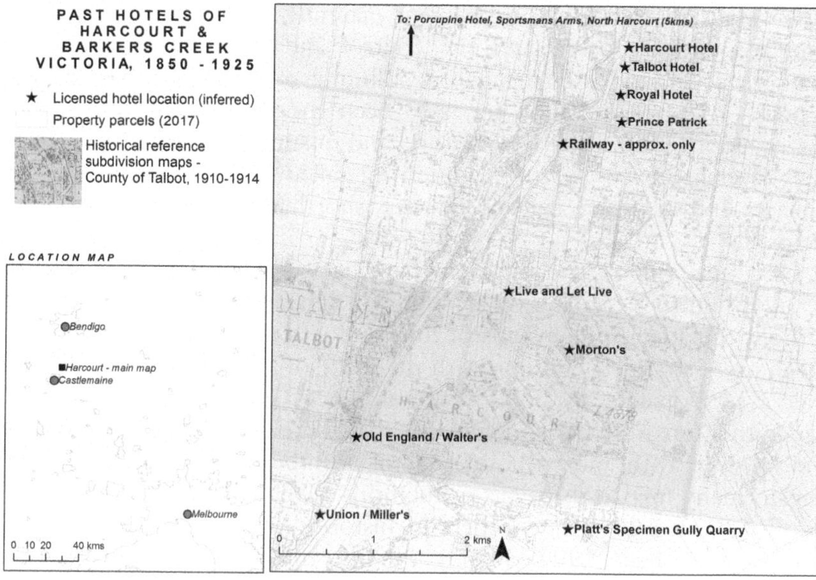

Fig. 1.1 Map of hotels past of Harcourt and Barkers Creek, Victoria

anti-alcohol temperance movement reshaped not only places like Harcourt and Barkers Creek, but the wider political landscape. I put forward a case that alcohol was one catalyst for the escalation and new forms of local level rights and controls during the late nineteenth and early twentieth centuries. Some of the traditions established through local alcohol controls crossed over with early zoning and continue to be recognisable in land use planning today. While the book is about rights and controls applicable to private land, its focus overlaps sometimes with the better-studied history of controls on drinking and drunkenness in public spaces.

The state of Victoria and its capital city Melbourne are the focus: these are places with their own idiosyncrasies but also broadly representative of trends in several other jurisdictions. I use archival records and historical Geographic Information System (GIS) techniques to support a review of the workings and debates of Victoria's early controls on the location and density of alcohol outlets, and their corollaries statutory limits and dry zones—some of which survive in residual form today. In so doing I show the temperance movement of the late nineteenth and early twentieth century using nascent planning laws to legitimise local popular political power, and the control and exclusion not only of alcohol but of land uses defined as polluting or disorderly. These local politics of the temperance era have been mostly overlooked in popular memory, and in urban history and planning scholarship: seemingly overshadowed by the notoriety of failed national prohibition in America and—in Australia—of *wowsers* (shorthand for grimly meddling teetotallers).

Of course, one reason they may have been overlooked is the level of detail of statutory controls on alcohol, which is overbearing enough even without the added dimensions of time and space. Researching the topic (beginning, strangely enough, with the study of a 2012 planning dispute over a McDonald's fast food restaurant—see Chapter 5), I soon realised with a mix of dread and curiosity that there is no clean break before and after, or with and without, alcohol prohibition—instead that there remain many myriad "smaller prohibitions" (Valverde 1998). Following Booth (2002, 2005), and others in historical studies of planning and related laws (Baar 1992; Blandy 2006; Brinkley and Vitiello 2013; Dennis 2000; DePastino 2010; Fischel 2004; Foglson 2005; Meyer and Brown 1989; Schilling and Linton 2005; Shumsky and Springer 1981), I pursued the idea that the genealogy of statutory details and rights applicable to alcohol and location have had real influence, and that they say something of the forces that created them. I use a legal history perspective—looking at the history of "planning before planning", of what Booth (2005) terms the nature of difference in traditions of law and government. And I focus on the language of rights—taking the view that asserted rights shape, and even create, cities (Staeheli and Mitchell 2008, p. 106 quoted in Attoh 2011, p. 673).

In this I have taken inspiration from Star (1999) who made "a call to study boring things"—to make unseen things visible, and to foreground the embedded histories of apparently neutral order. For this reason I pressed on in the research for this book, from lead to buried lead, through archives both digitised and paper, wary of falling into true bureaucratic or local obscurity but often on the precipice of it. The larger story I tell from this is of how the temperance movement, and the experiences and beliefs that fuelled it, influenced public policies and left legacies that continue to shape cities today. They also underscore the tensions and conflicts that define the futures of cities like Melbourne. Local option history still has legacies for, and parallels with, questions facing cities and planning policy. The early twenty-first century is a useful time to reflect on temperance history given that at the same time as some temperance era controls are being scaled back, essentially identical controls are being put forward for what appear to be much the same reasons. Far from being easily expunged remnants of wowserism, similar debates as around alcohol and local option in the late nineteenth and early twentieth centuries continue to spring up: reflecting basic tensions around to what extent local collective rights are an extension of individual and property rights, or a threat to them.

The book is set out as follows:

- Chapter 2 (The Talbot Hotel) looks at what the temperance movement of the late nineteenth and early twentieth centuries stood for and against, and the social forces that propelled it. It examines the relationships between the temperance movement, liberalism and property rights: how and why the temperance movement took an interest in *local* controls including on private land. It then reviews the rights and controls around alcohol that resulted, focusing on the often-overlooked spread of direct local democratic "local option" policies in several countries including Australia.
- Chapter 3 (The Live and Let Live Hotel) analyses the rise and influence of local controls on alcohol in Victoria from the 1860s. Beginning with early veto and local option provisions, the chapter tracks freezes on license numbers combined with voluntary polls, the License Reduction Board, and culminates in the 1920 statewide local option poll and the resultant dry zones. It maps the results of the poll, and considers how factors such as religion, and the boundaries of the poll, may have influenced results.
- Chapter 4 (The Old England Hotel) critically reviews the hangovers—legacies—of temperance and local option for systems of land use control today. These range from Melbourne's idiosyncratic dry zones and anti-alcohol covenants; to more intrinsic ideas of residential amenity and zoning; norms of separation; and the rights of residential property owners.
- In Chapter 5 (The Highland Society), I reflect on current conflicts in liquor licensing and planning. I argue that the local responses to alcohol that escalated during the temperance era are part of the foundations of planning, and the same tensions between individual and local rights underscore newer debates at the local level—for

example, around electronic gaming machines and "big box" bottle shops. They illustrate ongoing tensions between localism and centralism; age-old paradoxes around the promise and perils of majority democratic rights; and the persistence of domestic violence. I argue that looking at alcohol regulations in aspatial ways misrepresents their basic workings and histories, and that reflecting on this past contains lessons for policy today.

- Chapter 6 concludes with an epilogue revisiting Jack Wilkinson in Harcourt and Barkers Creek, many decades later and not long after the last pub had closed.

References

Attoh, K. A. (2011). What kind of right is the right to the city? *Progress in Human Geography, 35*(5), 669–685.

Baar, K. (1992). The national movement to halt the spread of multifamily housing, 1890–1926. *Journal of the American Planning Association, 58*(1), 39–48.

Blandy, S. (2006). Gated communities in England: Historical perspectives and current developments. *GeoJournal, 66*(1), 15–26.

Booth, P. (2002). From property rights to public control: The quest for public interest in the control of urban development. *Town Planning Review, 73*(2), 153–170.

Booth, P. (2005). The nature of difference: Traditions of law and government and their effects on planning in Britain and France. In B. Sanyal (Ed.), *Comparative planning cultures* (pp. 259–284). London: Routledge.

Brinkley, C., & Vitiello, D. (2013). From farm to nuisance: Animal agriculture and the rise of planning regulation. *Journal of Planning History*. https://doi.org/10.1177/1538513213507542.

Carr, H. A. (2002). *Bridging the generations: The story of Harcourt*. Maryborough, VIC: McPherson Printing Group.

Dennis, R. (2000). 'Zoning' before zoning: The regulation of apartment housing in early twentieth century Winnipeg and Toronto. *Planning Perspectives, 15*, 267–299.

DePastino, T. (2010). *Citizen hobo: How a century of homelessness shaped America*. Chicago: University of Chicago Press.

Fischel, W. A. (2004). An economic history of zoning and a cure for its exclusionary effects. *Urban Studies, 41*(2), 317–340.

Fogelson, R. (2005). *Bourgeois nightmares: Suburbia, 1870–1930*. New Haven, CT: Yale University Press.

Houston, P. (2009). *A pub on every corner series: Bendigo & surrounds* (Vol. 2). Licenses Reduction Board 1910.

Meyer, W. B., & Brown, M. (1989). Locational conflict in a nineteenth-century city. *Political Geography Quarterly, 8*(2), 107–122.

Public Records Office Victoria (PROV)—Series 515 (Central register of male prisoners), 19481.

Schilling, J., & Linton, L. S. (2005). The public health roots of zoning: In search of active living's legal genealogy. *American Journal of Preventive Medicine, 28*(2), 96–104.

Shumsky, N. L., & Springer, L. M. (1981). San Francisco's zone of prostitution, 1880–1934. *Journal of Historical Geography, 7*(1), 71–89.

Star, S. L. (1999). The ethnography of infrastructure. *American Behavioral Scientist, 43*(3), 377–391.

Staeheli, L., Mitchell, D. (2008). *The People's Property: Power, Politics and the Public.* New York: Routledge.

Valverde, M. (1998). *Diseases of the will: Alcohol and the dilemmas of freedom.* Cambridge and New York: Cambridge University Press.

Newspaper Articles

"The smash at Morley's Freemasons hotel", *Mount Alexander Mail,* April 24, 1863.

"Obscene language", *Mount Alexander Mail,* April 5, 1864.

"A rough customer", *Mount Alexander Mail,* April 25, 1874.

"Window breaking", *Mount Alexander Mail,* December 11, 1874.

"Assault", *Mount Alexander Mail,* April 17, 1878.

"Police court", *Bendigo Advertiser,* Saturday August 12, 1882, p. 2.

"A Harcourt pioneer", *The Bendigonian,* August 25, 1914, p. 27.

CHAPTER 2

The Talbot Hotel, 1883: A Tavern in the (Teetotal) Town

Abstract Opening with the story of the Talbot Hotel in Harcourt, central Victoria, which was closed then re-opened as an alcohol-free Coffee Palace, in this chapter Taylor describes the emergence and influence of the anti-alcohol temperance movement of the late nineteenth and early twentieth centuries. With international examples but focusing on Australia, Taylor characterises temperance groups and beliefs, highlighting the sometimes-surprising roles of Liberal ideals, and of responses to domestic violence. While temperance influence is better known for failed national prohibition, Taylor shows alliances earlier converging on calls for local rights, and argues democratic vetos on alcohol have had lasting but overlooked legacies. The chapter considers liquor licensing within the historical context of local laws, property rights and voting rights; pointing to shifts accompanying industrialization and suburbanization. It concludes by examining features of Local Option, Local Veto, and Permissive Bill policies including in Canada, the US, New Zealand, Scotland and Australia.

Keywords Temperance · Prohibition · Planning history · Localism Local option · Property rights

The Talbot Hotel in Harcourt, a small town in central Victoria, was licensed to sell alcohol from 1854 to 1883. It was then purchased by Hugh McLean, a teetotaller who proceeded to rip out its pipes and

© The Author(s) 2019

E. J. Taylor, *Dry Zones*, https://doi.org/10.1007/978-981-13-2787-2_2

publicly pour its stocks of liquor down the gutter. From then until its demolition in the 1950s, what had been the Talbot Hotel operated as an alcohol-free Coffee Palace: and while the township of Harcourt had once had as many as 6 hotels (see Fig. 1.1) the Talbot had been its last. Thereafter, Harcourt seemed to boast of its voluntary alcohol-free status. A complimentary visitor in 1901 recounted, in a newspaper travel column, how:

> The residents of Harcourt are nearly all teetotallers, and a fine temperance hotel and coffee palace has been built for the accommodation of visitors. There are no hotels, and what is better still, I was informed by the people, that, being nearly all Rechabites, and being no demand for alcohol, the supply ran out with the closing of the only hotel many years ago. ("Macedon and Harcourt: Harcourt a Voluntary Temperance Settlement", *The Bendigo Independent*, March 29, 1901, p. 3)

Harcourt may have had "a statewide reputation" for its voluntary pub closing efforts, but its experiences of the temperance movement—a set of values, beliefs, and policies framed in opposition to alcohol—were not isolated. Particularly during the later decades of the nineteenth century, the temperance movement swelled from a comparatively novel personal ethos that drinking spirits slightly less than always—being "temperate"—was a worthy idea, into a general opposition to alcohol (capital Tee-Total abstinence, or teetotalism), and into a formidable social movement and political force.

The ways temperance gained ground leveraged other, sometimes surprising, ideals of the late nineteenth century: private property rights; liberalism; municipalisation; and voting rights (enfranchisement). Combined with the more familiar moral and health arguments that temperance proponents waged against alcohol, such broader ideals converged, as this chapter sets out, on *local option* in liquor licensing. This chapter summarises what the temperance movement stood for and against, before looking at the ways temperance approached alcohol specifically in the context of place and local control—of the tavern (to reference the traditional folk song), in the town ("There is a Tavern in the Town", later rereleased as "The Drunkard's Song"). The chapter describes the influence of temperance and the spread across several countries of local, spatially defined vetos on private liquor sales—typically termed *local option*.

2.1 A Temperance Carol

In Charles Dickens' *A Christmas Carol: In Prose, Being a Ghost Story* the miserly central character, Scrooge, is visited by three spectres: the ghosts of Christmases past, present, and yet to come. Each ghost brings with it largely unwelcome insights into Scrooge's character. Much like the temperance movement, Dickens (and the word *Dickensian*, evoking the worlds of his books) seems intrinsically tied to the nineteenth century. Yet both Dickens and temperance have left long, faint tails. *A Christmas Carol* was first published in 1843 and not only popularised but, in some cases, as in the greeting "Merry Christmas!", literally invented much of the enduring Western iconography of Christmas celebrations. Trace a line back from the non-alcoholic Maisons sparkling grape drinks at the Christmas tables of my childhood, to my lifetime non-drinking mother signing the Order of Rechabites' "Temperance Physiology Examination" in 1958 Castlemaine, and on, and it is not so long before you arrive at the Methodist Church in the peak era of temperance activity, during which my forbearers in and around Harcourt were alternately assaulting publicans with fence palings, running hotels, and joining anti-alcohol religious orders. Measured in years, the temperance era as it played out in a relatively recently colonised Australia can seem so long ago as to be an abstract curiosity. Measured in generations, it is not so far removed.

The temperance movement itself is a well-documented topic. Accounts of the spread of temperance beliefs and policies in Australia can be found in *Wowsers* (Dunstan 1968); *A Rum State* (Lewis 1991); *Beyond the Ladies Lounge* (Wright 2014); parts of the edited volume *The Outcasts of Melbourne* (Davison et al. 1985); and others. Dingle (1980) gives an in-depth analysis of the politics of prohibition in England. Nicholls (2006, 2011) documents the longer-term politics of alcohol in the UK. Merrett (1979) details the activities of liquor licensing authorities through the early and mid twentieth century in Victoria. Valverde (1998), with a focus on Ontario and Canada, dissects shifts over time in beliefs about alcohol, and accompanying regulatory regimes. McNamara and Quilter (2015) trace shifts in public drinking controls in New South Wales including through the late nineteenth century. Here, I roughly summarise the groups active in the temperance movement, and the ways they framed alcohol as a problem.

Recognisably temperance ideas and groups originated in social movements of the UK in the 1830s, and were initially concerned with the moderated consumption of alcohol, usually spirits. Wine by contrast was often associated with sobriety and with advances in colonisation. Earlier connotations of "temperance" had referred to moderated food and drink consumption more generally—see Williamson (1992, p. 324). Temperance groups soon morphed into Total Abstinence principles formalised through Temperance and Total Abstinence societies. In Australia, the New South Wales Temperance Society was established in 1835, visiting Quakers formed the Port Phillip Temperance Society in Melbourne in 1837, the Melbourne Total Abstinence Society was founded in 1842, the Australia Felix Total Abstinence Society in 1845, and The Temperance League of Victoria in 1857. The temperance movement in Australia encompassed such groups as the Independent Order of Rechabites, Band of Hope, Sons of Temperance, Good Templars, the Methodist Church, Women's Christian Temperance Union (WCTU), Salvation Army, Blue Ribbon Army, and the Quaker church—"just" as Dunstan (1968) sardonically observed in *Wowsers*, "to mention a few" (p. 56).

Temperance encompassed nonconformist churches, particularly Methodists who made up a large part of Victoria's goldfields population. Lay preachers, auto didacticism, and civic reform ideals had strong roles in the Methodist church. Some religious groups, such as Quakers, saw temperance as part of a broader reform agenda and the campaign against slavery. Temperance gained adherents through lodges and friendly societies that offered income protection to temperate members at a time predating social welfare. The Good Templars, Independent Order of Rechabites, and Independent Order of Oddfellows Manchester Unity are examples; some have morphed into financial institutions. Some temperance campaigners from labour perspectives saw the liquor industry as exploitative, and campaigned for prohibitions on alcohol from a utopian, radical working class standpoint (Nicholls 2006, p. 139). As in parts of my family, temperance could function as social leverage: sobriety as a point of class distinction or mobility. The Salvation Army in particular drew its ranks from the lower classes of urban dwellers, and in Australia engaged in quite literal wars against slum conditions and gangs (Ussher 1985). The Salvation Army was built up using "countless narratives", writes Valverde (1998):

> …many of them autobiographical, of ordinary poor people driven to drink by poverty, by domestic violence, by seduction and abandonment, or by other everyday traumas of the urban poor. (Valverde 1998, p. 89)

Other aspects of the temperance movement came firmly from capital and the establishment, and operated in commercial spheres, with powerful proponents in industry—including Quaker chocolate families (Cadbury 2011) and temperance-espousing property developers such as James Munro, Melbourne Temperance Party leader, and land boom developer. As well as suburban real estate development and speculation, Munro was a developer of Coffee Palaces and Temperance Hotels: elaborate alcohol-free hotels built to compete with licensed venues using coffee and waitresses. Harcourt's Coffee Palace was a modest example of this trend, which reached its peak in the 1880s alongside the land boom.

Temperance groups were active in fostering alternative social infrastructure: sometimes as at small and practical a level as public water fountains, but through to large-scale housing provision in the development of early model towns, cooperative and subsidised housing, and social research (as in the Rowntree trusts). The Rowntree and Cadbury chocolatier families built their model worker towns, Bourneville and New Earswick, as dry (alcohol-free) estates and as examples through to which to influence public policy thinking. Earlier Quaker industrial families in Ireland built Bessbrook along Temperance rules (Williamson 1992, p. 318). Temperance Institution established free libraries and public temperance halls, and were, as Lewis (1991) summarised, "infected with the general optimism of the period concerning social advance" while reflecting "a larger disquiet about the extent of poverty and the role of drink in its spread". An interest in reform and improvement of working and housing conditions both in themselves, and as a means of combatting alcohol, underscored much of this work.

A further force in temperance was the WCTU. Often understood as representing proto-feminist politics, the WCTU was established in 1873 in the United States, with branches in Australia from 1887. The WCTU and other groups engaged in direct protests against licensed premises. Women were, on the whole, excluded from such venues—especially from the "saloons" of the United States where a key prohibitionist alliance was the "Anti-Saloon League". In Australia, significant numbers of women ran hotels and were afforded an unconventional degree of autonomy in doing so, making gender divisions around the spaces of alcohol less clear (as explored in detail by Wright 2014). The WCTU and other campaigners mobilised temperance around an appeal for women's rights as defined by rigid gender roles. They were instrumental in the push for women's suffrage, and in the early suffrage achieved in New Zealand and South

Australia. For many, the stated goal of attaining votes for women was to attain votes against liquor licenses, and in so doing protect traditional family institutions (Dannenbaum 1981, p. 240).

Physical violence, particularly violence by men against women in the home, was not the central focus of the temperance movement, but it was far from peripheral to it. The "special burden borne by the wives of inebriates" was a central concern of all temperance reformers (Dannenbaum 1981), and a recurrent theme in temperance literature. References to violence in the home are common in temperance literature, with varying degrees of directness. As one example, an American cartoon from 1871 shows a man next to an overturned table in a bleak room, holding a screaming woman by the front of her clothes and attempting to punch her. Frightened children and a neighbour try to pull him off. The cartoon is captioned "quarrels between Mr. and Mrs. Latimer, and brutal violence between them, were the natural consequences of the too frequent use of the bottle" (Library of Congress Prints 1871). In contrast to twenty-first-century policy narratives associating *public* drinking with threats of street violence, public drunkenness controls in the temperance era were more focussed on moral disorder, and "sweeping" degenerate people from public view on amenity grounds (McNamara and Quilter 2015).

Given that at other points in history violence in the home had been largely condoned, Pleck (1989) attributes a sudden interest in domestic violence during the temperance movement to growing fears about public criminality and immorality, with concerns children from abusive homes would add up to waves of disorder (p. 36). Tomes (1978), drawing on detailed London courts records, found a shift in social and legal attitudes towards domestic violence as reflected in magistrates' rulings during the temperance era: with wife beating repositioned as an indicator of a failure of men to be "natural protectors". Such framing was apparent in an 1885 Victorian petition for local option, presented to the Victorian Parliament by the Victorian Alliance for Local Option and signed by 45,000 women. The petition referenced "cruel" behaviour against women by men "from whom they should receive protection", but who had been "made brutal" by liquor (1885 Local Option Alliance petition, quoted in Dunstan 1968, p. 104).

A cursory glance through nineteenth-century newspapers from Victoria shows that the John "Jack" Wilkinson mentioned at the start of this book was far from the first violent and drunk man mused upon by colonial authorities. An early commentator on Melbourne claims that amongst the very first liquor licensing rules in what was then the Colony of Port Phillip, in 1838, held that:

> ...if a publican sold liquor to a married person whose intemperance was known to be of injury to his family he was liable to a penalty of 5 pounds. (Garryowen quoted in Weidenhoffer 1967, p. 33)

The first person executed in the newly formed Colony of Victoria was Patrick Kennedy, in 1851. Coincidentally, in the same newspaper as John "Jack" Wilkinson's sentencing, the *Castlemaine Mail* of 11 November 1882, was a reprinted article about the 1851 murder Patrick Kennedy was hanged for, headed "A Shocking Wife Murder". This recalled how Kennedy had murdered his wife Mary in the Western District of Victoria in the earliest days of the colony. Kennedy had kicked and beaten Mary with a shepherd's crook after disappointment with her cooking. The article featured extensive descriptions of the amount of rum consumed in the lead-up to the murder. Kennedy "was usually a good tempered man", a witness stated, but the rum "seemed to put him into something more, and set him crazy". The judge, passing sentence of death, remarked that:

> Almost every serious offence sprung from this source (intemperance). Indeed, I cannot remember a single crime of any magnitude but what could be traced to drunkenness. I beg of all present who are pursuing the drunkard's career, and sneer at any remonstrance that might be urged upon them, to take warning by the present example. ("A Shocking Wife Murder", *Castlemaine Mail*, November 11, 1882, p. 4)

The warnings of prominent Melbourne temperance campaigner, E.W. Cole, in "The Evils of the Drink Traffic", likewise drew links between alcohol and violence and disorder in the home (even with references to butchering and massacres):

> It makes wives widows, children orphans, fathers fiends...It fills your jails, supplies your alms houses, and demands your asylums. It engenders controversies, fosters quarrels, and cherishes riots. It crowds your penitentiaries and furnishes the victims for your scaffolds...It incites the father to butcher his helpless offspring, helps the husband to massacre his wife, and aids the child to grind the parricidal axe. (E.W. Cole on "The Evils of the Drink Traffic", quoted in Dunstan 1968, pp. 35–36)

Men who drank, temperance logic went, beat their wives, and occasionally murdered their entire families. They were defective as workers and as family heads. Equivalent social concerns around women and alcohol focused on fears of contamination (moral and physical), and the neglect of children and family structures. Temperance campaigners expressed concerns women who drank neglected their children, had defective children, or became "fallen" women by having sex or children outside of social and legal structures, for example as prostitutes or unmarried mothers. "Habitual drunkard" and "inebriates" laws around public drinking were targeted at, and disproportionately used to incarcerate, women, as well as being used disproportionately against poor and Indigenous people. In the early twentieth century concern about women and alcohol refocussed on eugenics and race decline and saw a successful campaign to "to remove children (and hence housewives) from licensed premises". At that point the science was hazy but the social position on women and alcohol agreed that:

> Whether one believed that drunken mothers were a national curse because their behaviour was passed on to future generations or simply because they were bad mothers, middle-class social observers could agree that maternal drinking was a terrible thing. Either way, through defective germ plasm or though vice, drunken mothers ended up with dead infants and defective children. (Valverde 1998, p. 54)

The narratives in each—violent man, fallen woman—had smatterings of medicalisation but were weighted by fears of social disorder. Valverde characterises policy approaches to alcohol as hybrids swinging between moral and incomplete scientific rationales, and structured around compelling if unstated social narratives. Within the temperance movement the idea that alcohol stood for misery—a loose association of poverty, violence, suicide, ill health and disorder—was a key part of temperance narratives, including around the decline of Harcourt's hotels. The last licensee of The Porcupine Inn in North Harcourt, for example, Charles Salsbury, had mortgaged the property and lost most of the family's assets in pursuit of a business venture. He had taken on the hotel after marrying Mary, widow of former licensee Edward Martin, five years previously. In 1864, with bailiffs closing in, Mary apparently drowned herself in the nearby reservoir, "in distress of mind about losing the property". At the autopsy, one of her children deposed that their stepfather was often "unkind" to their mother—"calling her names, blackening her eye, bleeding her nose, striking and stunning her". This in itself was not recorded as remarkable, merely mentioned as a caveat to the fact Mary's son "never heard Salsbury threaten his mother". Thus her death was not considered suspicious, merely squalid. Newspapers evoked "a depression of spirits and a horror of the whole picture" at the scene of Mary Salsbury's death, and assigned the whole "mournful proceedings" to alcohol (specifically to "intemperate excesses and their inevitable train of retributive miseries"):

> The head of the family hiding himself from a host of creditors, the young children looking on hopelessly and despairingly, while on a miserable stretcher in a dark chamber, lies stretched the stiffened corpse of the mother, who, crushed in mind and body by the result of *intemperate excesses and their inevitable train of retributive miseries*, has put an end to her life in a moment of frenzy! ("Suicide at the Porcupine", *Mount Alexander Mail*, Monday April 11, 1864, p. 3, emphasis added)

The joyfully outraged reporting of suicides and other matters covered by Police and Coroner's courts was common for newly popularised newspapers of the time—the collection by Michael Lesy in *Wisconsin Death Trip* is another example. The Porcupine never reopened. It had closed for financial reasons but, as the next chapter details, from 1865 onwards the barriers to opening hotels in Victoria began to tighten. Temperance forces not only built the coffee palaces and other institutions of an alternative social order. They also applied themselves to destroying the institutions of alcohol: influencing liquor licensing and other legislation to make it harder to open hotels, easier to close them, and much in between subject to checks and controls.

2.2 Alcohol and the State: Close Enemies

The temperance movement did not *create* controls on alcohol—trade in alcoholic drinks had been regulated for several centuries in the English system inherited in its colonies. Alcohol in the English tradition has long been both controlled and facilitated centrally by governments. Smith (1982) goes so far as saying that "historically, regulation of the alcoholic beverage industry is as old as government itself". However, divisions between drinking and non-drinking situations were rarely sharply made until the temperance era: distilled drinks have often been safer than water; and wine and beer widely drunk even while puritan viewpoints viewed overconsumption of hard liquor negatively. Public drunkenness has been criminalised both before and after the temperance era, although the rationales for these controls have shifted.

From its earliest years, the Victorian colony inherited essentially all its laws—including liquor licensing—from England and from the penal world of New South Wales, with a licensing system overseen by magistrates (see Lewis 1991; Nicholls 2011). Australia's early liquor licensing laws uneasily combined the protection of oligarchical business interests, with avoiding the social disorder associated with alcohol, and avoiding the inverse social disorder associated with regulating alcohol too punitively. Lewis (1991) in "*A Rum State*" emphasised the often-contradictory relationships between government and alcohol in Australian colonial history, with governments both profiteering from alcohol, and involved in moral panics about its use particularly of hard spirits (see also Gilling 2016). Earlier, England's "gin craze" of the eighteenth century was directly facilitated by licensing and tariff changes designed to undercut imported French brandy. The moral panic that followed—focused on crime, urban drinking, and drinking by women (Herring et al. 2008)—prompted further licensing changes. In such examples central state controls, and social practices of alcohol, are self-reflective: it is difficult to disentangle one from the other.

A necessary if obvious distinction to make is between licensing and prohibition: many religious (Islamic) countries maintain outright criminal prohibitions on alcohol. By contrast, liquor licensing, the primary legislative means through which alcohol is controlled in the Anglosphere, is a state function through which rights to manufacture or sell alcohol are conditionally granted. While some aspects of alcohol control are subject to criminal law, licensing is based on issuing or withdrawing rights subject to conditions and fees. Licensing also typically goes hand in hand with taxation usually, with alcohol, in the form of excises based on the strength of alcohol sold. In practice, licensing confers a grant of freedoms subject to conditions, and is in effect a restraint more than a right.

Some distinctions between prohibition and licensing control are seen after the repeal of prohibition in Ontario, for example, when a complex web of licensing and street level regulations took its place—with license inspectors closely monitoring the furniture, music, and food of venues (Valverde 1998, p. 159). A similar move from criminalised to licensed and zoned activity occurred around prostitution (legalised in Victoria in the 1980s); and is underway in US states where medical or medicinal forms of cannabis has recently been legalised (McComas 2016; Németh and Ross 2014; Salkin and Kansler 2010). In the Anglosphere and Northern European countries and their colonies alcohol has always been, for practical purposes, subject to some form of licensing and associated controls. Public drinking or drunkenness has also always been subject to some level of control, and in the early days of the NSW colony accounted for around 60% of arrests—functioning as a form of control on public order and amenity (McNamara and Quilter 2015). These are in contrast with outright prohibition, and with the more permissive regimes around trading and consuming alcohol in, for example, many southern European countries. State monopoly systems are also common forms of control: state monopoly sales (especially of heavier alcoholic beverages) are maintained in several Scandinavian countries; most Canadian provinces; and 17 US states.

In the United States and other countries, a coalition of temperance interests came together in campaigns for forms of prohibition on alcohol from the early 1850s, gaining political traction in many countries by the end of the nineteenth century. The peak of political influence of the temperance movement is commonly remembered as an almost monumentally misguided national policy—total prohibition in the United States through the 1919 Volstead Act. In Australia, the high (or low) water mark of temperance influence is understood to be a significant change to liquor licensing legislation—the introduction of six o'clock hotel closing, which occurred in all Australian States during the First World War. Although intended to be a temporary patriotic measure (spurred on by King George, and by incidents with drunken troops), the "six o'clock swill"—the crush of heavy drinking by men in public bars between 5 p.m. knock off and 6 p.m. closing—was to be an institution defining utilitarian drinking cultures in the State of Victoria, into the 1960s (Phillips 1980; Oldham 2013).

Temperance politics in Australia became prominent in the 1870s and particularly 1880s, with two international temperance conventions held in Melbourne in 1880 and 1888. Australian temperance campaigners in their peak period of political influence sought a higher drinking age, weaker liquor, shorter hotel hours, Sunday closing, and to remove barmaids from hotels. They also sought and partly attained a greater local say in reducing hotel numbers and determining their locations. Campaigning for different scales of prohibition through local option type laws within the licensing legislation was once a focus issue for temperance in Australia.

Valverde (1998) characterises instruments of alcohol controls as having a focus on time, liquid, or space. Time-based elements of Australian liquor licensing (the six o'clock swill) have been comparatively well studied. Australia also long had, and retains, complex taxation laws around the liquid itself—alcohol excise, an important and debated source of central government revenue (Skov 2009). Overshadowed by the notoriety of national prohibition (and, in Australia, the spectres of the six o'clock swill and its attendant wowsers), the temperance era is not often remembered for its convoluted local-level politics. Yet local control and property rights had a role in the temperance movement and its influence. For much of its history temperance influence worked at far smaller scales than national. Neither Australia nor Victoria, saw total prohibition on alcohol of the kind once famously applied in the United States or as remains in many religious states today. Instead, in addition to restrictions on the times when and people for whom purchasing alcohol of differing strengths was legal, Victoria saw *local* prohibitions introduced on the places where alcohol could be served.

2.3 The Local: Something Borrowed, Something New

While controls on alcohol were not new, some principles of liquor licensing, including the notion that local communities ought to have the right to directly determine by whether and how alcohol was allowed in their area, newly took root during the temperance era. The nature of licensing control can be seen to shift during the nineteenth century in Australia, as in several other jurisdictions. One aspect of this shift was a move away from central and judicial, to local and democratic.

Just as the temperance movement did not invent alcohol control, neither did it invent local controls. It is useful to briefly consider what is meant here by *local*. *Local* in part refers to local government and to the rights of cities and municipalities to self-rule: to the very long traditions of self-rule of cities, towns and villages. A *by-law* is a locally defined, or city, law—the term in English is sometimes is assumed to mean "lesser" but its origins are in the Old Norse term *byr* (town) and later the Middle English *byrlaw* (local law or custom). A by-law is a rule established by a community to regulate itself. A more recent term, *localism*, has multiple often purposefully vague connotations (as detailed by

Clarke and Cochrane 2013) but at its simplest refers to the devolvement of government to smaller scales, within some form of hierarchy. Pratchett (2004) distinguishes local autonomy from local democracy and identity—each representing different aspects of local freedom *to* or freedom *from* central government.

Local also refers to borders—to keeping people in and out. There is a longer and more complex history of the *local*, which is in effect the genealogy of sovereignty and citizenship—the city-state, the burgher, liberties, *stadtluft macht frei* (city air makes you free), *communes*, and other traditions (see Isin 2002 for an exploration). For the purposes of this book it is enough to point out, as does Isin, that citizenship and democracy have always required (indeed, all but been defined by) borders, and the delineation of who is in and out. From the late nineteenth century onwards, US west coast states have had a focus on direct local democracy (Goebel 1997). Recent decades have seen a broader resurgence of ideals of direct local democracy and autonomy (Boudreau 2003).

In English and related traditions for centuries, criminal and related law—most obviously vagrancy and settlement laws—had explicit spatial powers and were key tools in powers of exclusion. These have always been disproportionately applied to poor and marginal groups. DePastino (2010) in *Citizen Hobo* related how localities in England, under the Poor Laws (and related Settlement Laws), and later in the American colonies "took vigorous measures to suppress the transient poor". Ironically, the English Poor Laws were intended to require local parishes to look after their own poor—with the perhaps inevitable effect that parishes were anxious to stop poor people other than "theirs" entering their boundaries. Through this legal tradition, tightly regulated towns could ban newcomers with unwanted religions, ideas, or moral standards. Transients could be deemed "vagabonds" and subject to corporal punishment:

> Settlement laws which remained in effect until well into the twentieth century, protected towns not only from the responsibilities of poor relief, but also from the exotic cultural influences that often accompanied wandering strangers…Like the laws of settlement, vagrancy statutes legitimized and facilitated the mobility of better-off transients while discouraging and criminalizing the movement of the poor. (DePastino 2010, p. 6)

Victoria in its early years criminalised vagrancy, with the 1852 Vagrant Act—formally defining and controlling the movements of "idle and disorderly persons" and "rogues and vagabonds"; as well as legislating against criminal migrants from Tasmania ("An Act to facilitate the apprehension and prevent the introduction into the Colony of Victoria of Offenders illegally at large", 1852, "An Act to prevent the influx of criminals into Victoria", 1854). Similarly in NSW, public drunkenness and associated vagrancy laws were a major and class-based focus of criminal law including through the nineteenth century. Over time, vagrancy and settlement laws softened to be about not allowing poor or criminal people to *stay*, and requiring them to "be genuinely looking for work". George Orwell in *Down and Out in Paris and London* describes moving from parish to parish to avoid staying more than one night, and thus being jailed for vagrancy. Orwell stated that the prevailing occupation of a tramp—the cause of his tramping, in fact—was in skirting the bureaucratic details of local laws.

Changing economic and political conditions through the nineteenth and twentieth centuries saw ever-larger numbers of mobile populations. Migration and individual rights have close inverse relationships with local laws: Garnett (2005) explores how laws concerned with disorder—suspected criminality, vagrancy, bars, prostitution—have always had spatial elements. Over the second half of the twentieth century, police powers around vagrancy and suspicion were scaled back amidst civil rights action particularly concerned with the civil liberties of black men. Garnett suggests that as civil liberties increased, the use of local land use policies to relocate disorder has correspondingly increased. Put another way, increases in individual rights tend to correspond to more place-based control of activities. Public drinking in Australia was decriminalised in the second half of the twentieth century, but regulatory techniques including local by-laws quickly emerged to fill the "void" (McNamara and Quilter 2015). The rise of exclusionary private covenants in late nineteenth-century America had been fairly openly framed both as a product of, and a defensive reaction to, the migration of blacks from the South. Enclosure acts (fencing of common areas) and trespassing legislation in the United States also escalated after the civil war.

In the nineteenth century, autocratic restrictions on individual freedom of movement and religion receded amidst industrialisation and reform, but contributed to a particular version of local control. *Municipalisation* was based on enfranchisement—voting—and on property and industry (The voting franchise in Britain began to expand through legislation from 1832 onwards). Municipal corporations represented the interests of their ratepayers—enfranchised property owners. While in principle allowing simply a delegation of powers to areas to manage the details of their own local affairs, in practice Booth (2005) traces a constant tension between local and central government introduced to the English system through the 1835 Municipal Corporations Act, which:

> … laid the foundation for an uneasy relationship between central government and local authorities, with local government clamouring for freedom to act in their own interests and central government being unsure as to how far and in what ways it should intervene in this local exercise of power. (Booth 2005, "The Nature of Difference")

The Liberal party was one of two major parties in the UK in the nineteenth to early twentieth centuries—it combined free trade, social reform, personal liberty, and reduction in crown and church powers. British Liberal leader William Vernon Harcourt is remembered for his phrase "we are all socialists now"—which, Hunt (2010) argues, referred to a nineteenth-century support for municipal-level collectivism widespread at the time in spite of antagonism to socialism more broadly (pp. 372–373). In Parliamentary discussions, Harcourt argued for local government at as small a scale as possible, emphasising the importance of locally specific policies. Another Liberal, John Stuart Mill, also wrote strongly in support of elected local governments—both as an opportunity for political participation; and because of a view of local governments as more efficient and effective than central government, on the basis of local knowledge, interest, and expertise (Andrew and Goldsmith 1998; Mill 1861).

Australia both as a colony and as a federation has not had a strong tradition of local governance or self-rule: being founded and largely ruled as a centralised penal colony. In the context of Australia, *local* typically came to be defined by the property rights of colonisation. Particularly with the advent of Torrens Title systems, land ownership and rights were mapped and allocated, and in so doing, dispossessed traditional Indigenous occupants of rights to land. In the settler colonial world, access to property was uneven, and property came with local enfranchisement and democratic rights: critical in the temperance movement. Local government itself has, however, rarely been a strong arm of government in Australia—while municipal corporations and shires existed from early in the colonies, they have typically managed mundane affairs and had comparatively limited autonomy. South Australia, the only Australian state without a convict history, had the strongest and earliest local government system (Robbins 1978) as well as originating the use of Torrens Title.

Australian local government is in some contrast to the United States, with a traditionally strong, rights-based level of local government. The right to self-rule of American states and municipalities is an important political principle in the United States. Home rule in the United States grants cities, municipalities, and counties the ability to pass laws to govern themselves as they see fit (within the bounds of the Constitution). Some US states are home rule states (with a fundamentalist approach to local rights), others have a modified local autonomy, known as "Dillon's Law" states. The federal structure of the US constitution was designed to avoid two perceived risks: the internal corruption and decline of large states, and the external vulnerability of small ones (drawing on Montesquieu—Bednar 2008).

Local community traditionally tended to mean a place to which people belonged by some birthright or religious affiliation, and to whose control they were more or less explicitly subject and confined. In the nineteenth century, and particularly in a colonial context, local community increasingly came to mean somewhere where property afforded a person rights including voting rights. It also came to carry a (slightly reimagined) idea of local and neighbourhood: based on civic ideals of freedom, democracy, and property rights but also on limits to private use of public land. The liberal ideals at work were that (certain) people have rights to vote; that property owners have rights (including to enjoy their properties, to be free from nuisance); that local areas have the right to determine the rules they live by; and to some extent also the responsibility to provide their own services and infrastructure.

As local option debates about alcohol would show, this version of *local* was not necessarily much less inclined to be exclusionary or repressive than the pitchfork-wielding village of old. Local laws are often—by their nature—exclusionary, and are sometimes racially exclusionary: a tension apparent in examples of US federal involvement in state and local laws. Racial zoning ordinances were common in American cities in the early twentieth century (Silver 1997). However, the US Supreme Court rejected explicit racial zoning in Buchanan v. Warley (1917). In the wake of judicial decisions against explicit racial zoning, racial zoning or similar ordinances resembling racial zoning became legally problematic. Fischel (2004, p. 330) argues that instead, exclusionary zoning mechanisms were devised to achieve the same objectives. US courts ruled against racial zoning (Cuchana v. Warley 1917) and later against exclusionary zoning (Mount Laurel 1975 and 1983 cases—see Silver 1997). School desegregation cases also played out the rights of state and local governments in the context of federal constitution also protecting individual rights. Local governments, local laws, and local rights have a vital but fraught role in the rights-based context that is modern liberal democracy.

2.4 Temperance and Local Control

Although liquor licenses are tied to specific places (most obviously hotels) and persons (licensees), until the advent of the temperance movement licensing systems rarely had an explicit interest in the location or neighbourhood in which alcohol was sold. At least insofar as promotional slogans (as in the Rechabites' "Temperance – Fortitude – Justice"), to some, temperance was a banner issue on a path towards broader social reform and justice and total prohibition was the end goal. Others were specifically interested in local place-based changes to liquor licensing legislation: to take into account the rights of residents, and to reflect variations in attitudes towards alcohol.

Place-based controls on alcohol have largely tended to be considered only as precursors (failed or otherwise) to total prohibition. Volk (2009), looking at the implications of local option for direct democracy is one exception, with a US perspective.

Some crossovers between temperance and the planning of space are well known: the social experiments and utopianism of the temperance movement and their legacies for planning were significant. Less explored are the principles of property and emergent planning law—in the context of municipalisation and suburbanisation—used to legitimise the use of political power in order to control private liquor activity. Model towns such as Bourneville were not just designed spaces but *controlled* spaces—with dryness a key component of how they were built and understood. The scales of activity through which this occurred relied less on centralised state control than on private property rights; and less on explicit moralisation than on asserted local democratic rights to exclude—in this case, alcohol—from particular places.

In the United States, the alcohol controls that culminated in national prohibition started with local and state laws. Hence long after the controversial Volstead Act, many US states and hundreds of US localities retained (or regained) their own prohibitions on alcohol. Technically, the repeal of the Volstead Act returned alcohol control to US states. Some retained prohibition; some introduced licensing systems; and some introduced state monopoly controls over alcohol sales (Alcoholic Beverage Control or ABC states—of which 17 remained in 2018).

In Victoria, forms of locally or spatially defined prohibition had been in place early on the Victorian goldfields over 1852–1854. Goldfields prohibition was introduced by Governor La Trobe who claimed "the illicit sales of liquor was the cause of nine tenths of the crime and disorder at the diggings"—echoing longer anxieties over convicts and crime in the Australian colonies. The policing of public drinking on grounds of controlling disorder and preserving public amenity had also long been standard in colonial Australia. Goldfields prohibition led to destructive standoffs over the proliferation of illegal alcohol sales ("sly grog"). By 1854 a Select Committee found the unintended consequences had been severe, and goldfields prohibition was removed, reverting to normal licensing requirements.

Another example of spatially defined prohibition by the state in Victoria was the City of Mildura (Victoria), which along with Renmark (South Australia), was founded as an alcohol-free settlement. The ban on alcohol sales was part of the Irrigation Act (1886). The irrigation system founders, the Chaffeys, had previously established a prohibition settlement in California. Designation as a dry city apparently meant problem drinkers were sent to Mildura—as in a letter quoted by Dunstan (1968)—"mother, Ernest is a drunkard. Our only hope is to send him to Mildura where he will be out of reach of alcohol" (p. 90).

Mildura's dry status was imposed externally and centrally, with the (possibly inevitable) consequence that locals went to no small effort to bypass the restrictions. Front "clubs" sprang up to supply, but officially not to publically sell, liquor, to circumvent the letter of the law. The dry phase was temporary and eventually converged with the complex local option laws described in following sections—Mildura initially was exempted from normal local option provisions until 1916 (with only club or wine licenses possible, and all requiring special colonial approval). After being included in local option in 1918, Mildura was divided into two licensing areas (Mildura West, and Merbein) and residents voted "wet" in 1918 and 1924 respectively. In the meantime, from the 1880s to 1910s, disorder apparently ensued, with Dunstan quoting a weary magistrate for Mildura as saying:

> The clubs supplied a large need, but it made a very bad beginning. I wish I could get out of mind the scenes and facts brought into my life. (Former Magistrate during Mildura's dry period, quoted in Dunstan 1968, p. 92)

Rather than externally imposed prohibition as in the goldfields and Mildura, temperance influence in Australia as elsewhere chiefly bought about other local mechanisms with which to limit sites for sale and consumption of alcohol. These more often relied on (a) private property rights (covenants); or (b) local by-laws; or (c) on escalating local political rights, themselves often based on property ownership; as means to exclude or minimise the number of liquor licenses nearby. These are each considered briefly before focusing on the third, in the form of local option.

Covenants are restrictions bound to property titles. In the late nineteenth and early twentieth century, before public zoning, private developers often introduced restrictive covenants to residential land sales. Typical private covenants in temperance era Victoria stipulated building materials, limited building density and dwelling numbers, and prohibited the sale or manufacture of alcohol (Taylor and Rowley 2017). Some were explicitly anti-alcohol and introduced by estate developers influential in the temperance movement. An example of alcohol-related covenants applies in a segment of Ascot Vale, a suburb in the north west of Melbourne, developed in 1886–1887 with covenants holding that:

> No building is to be erected on the land included in any purchase hereunder shall be used for a Brewery, Distillery, Public House or other place for the sale, storage or manufacture of spirituous or fermented liquor.

That area, bound by Union, Epsom and Maribyrnong Roads, is known as the "Temperance Triangle". Another area with anti-alcohol covenants in Victoria is the seaside area of Ocean Grove, first subdivided and developed as a Coffee Palace and holiday resort by the Methodist Church in the 1880s. The land comprised an alcohol-free Coffee Palace, with surrounding land covered by covenants on title prohibiting the sale or manufacture of alcohol. In addition to specifically temperance-based covenants, at least some general residential covenants from the late nineteenth and early twentieth centuries also excluded hotels—the subdivision of Moreland in 1882 by Montague Dare, for example, includes a covenant "banning shops, hotels, or low-value housing". Others, for example, in Ivanhoe excluded "immoral activities". Restrictive covenants on property titles limited alcohol sales by private contract and were sold as a feature of residential subdivisions.

Local by-laws and, previously, criminal law, has often banned or limited the consumption of alcohol in public spaces. This book is more focused on regulations of private land, however by-laws controlling alcohol consumption escalated, in Victoria, through changes to local government legislation in the early twentieth century (particularly the 1915 *Local Government Act*). Public drinking laws have functioned as spatial ordering or "sweeping", in that they usually target forms of drinking considered disorderly. Alcohol by-laws typically ban alcohol consumption or limit it to certain times and conditions consistent with local norms of civilised drinking. Studies of public alcohol by-laws highlight their function as a normative control on disorder and delinquency (Atkinson 2003; Jayne et al. 2011), and disproportionate use against some groups, for example, in Australia, Indigenous people (Pennay and Room 2012; Langton 1993; McNamara and Quilter 2015).

2.5 Think Globally, Act Local (Option)

While covenants and by-laws were important in temperance era controls on alcohol, this book is focused on the third element as listed above: direct democratic local controls on liquor license numbers and locations.

Local option in Australia and Victoria came in the context of similar ideas across several countries in the late nineteenth century. The trend was partly facilitated by emergent ideals of municipal control: for example, in Britain, Liberal leader Harcourt likened liquor control to sanitation in what Hunt (2010) characterises as municipal socialism or collectivism—and proposed basing local option on sanitation districts ("Local Option in England", *South Australian Register*, June 30, 1883). At a time when property owners and municipalities were ascendant, temperance proponents of local option emphasised the gradual and democratic features of democratic vetos on liquor licenses.

Alcohol was one catalyst for municipal controls in the nineteenth century—responses to migration and industrialisation were others. Proponents of local option also emphasised the efficacy of policies tailored to local circumstances: how prohibition could be "adopted wherever the condition of a favourable local sentiment existed" (Dingle 1980, p. 17). Helped by such packaging, over the late nineteenth and early twentieth centuries a fashion for local option spread seemingly in large part by referring to validating examples elsewhere. So while the Australian press reported on local option in England, in England in 1906 successes in the colonies were cited in Parliament, as in an Act proposing:

> That this House notes with satisfaction the successful working of the local option laws in the colonies, and approves the principle on which these laws are based, namely, that the people ought to possess, through a vote of the local electors, the power to protect themselves against the admitted evils of the Liquor Traffic. (Dingle 1980, p. 112)

Forms of local prohibitions were instigated in the USA, Canada, UK, New Zealand, Denmark, Finland, Norway, and Sweden over the late nineteenth and early twentieth centuries (see Table 2.1 for a summary of examples of local option policies by country). They were known variously as Local Option, Local Veto, or Permissive Bills. Rowntree published regularly on temperance and social issues, documenting the use of such statutory controls (e.g. Rowntree and Sherwell 1899). The principles of local option held that local people—which usually meant ratepayers, which usually meant property owners—ought to have the democratic right to decide by popular vote whether and to what extent to have liquor outlets in their area.

Broadly, local option gave voters direct popular vote on local alcohol policies, licensing numbers, or individual decisions. This was presented both as a form of direct democracy, and as a liberal approach to managing the social costs of alcohol. Local option proponents claimed that local residents (variously defined, but often ratepayers) of local areas (variously defined) ought to have the right to decide whether and to what extent alcohol could be sold in their area. This accorded with liberal and municipal rights-based ideals. Rowntree and Sherwell (1899) emphasised that whereas total prohibition in the UK was unfeasible, local opinion was still appealing as its principle was that it would apply only where popular sentiment supported it. This typically meant religious and rural areas, as in:

Table 2.1 Local option prohibition laws—examples by country

Country	*Local option prohibition laws on alcohol*
United States	"Maine Law"—named for the State of Maine which first became dry in 1851. Other dry states late nineteenth–early twentieth century: Kansas, Vermont, North and South Dakota, Oklahoma, Alabama, Georgia The culmination of states, counties, and towns as dry areas led to the campaign for national prohibition and 1919 Volstead Act. Local option valorised as ultimate democracy, and criticised as ultimate despotism (Volk 2009). Underpinned by local and state rights—"home rule" Dry states, counties, and towns remained after the 1933 national repeal. In 2016, 33 US states retained local option provisions, and in 3 states counties were dry by default. Hundreds of dry areas remain: e.g. in Kansas and Kentucky. 17 retain state monopolies on alcohol sales
United Kingdom	Intended to be devolved and permissive of local variation—named the Permissive Bill. Proposed only (except Scotland). Would have granted "areas" (counties, boroughs, wards, sanitary districts, etc.) rights of local veto to reduce liquor licenses with a two-thirds majority *Permissive Prohibitory Intoxicating Liquors Bill* first proposed 1864. Versions of the Permissive Bill defeated seven times including 1895 *Intoxicating Liquors Traffic Local Control Bill*. The Peel Commission (1869–1899) proposed statutory limits on hotels—also not introduced. The Permissive Bill issue split the Liberal Party between defenders of local liberties and individual liberties. Some dry areas in the UK exist via private covenants or similar
(Scotland)	Local option introduced to Scotland via the Temperance (Scotland) Act 1913. Supported by strong liberal and temperance traditions. First votes in 1920 with a choice of continuance, abolition, or 25% reduction. Between 1913 and 1965, 1131 polls were held. By 1970, 16 dry districts remained. Local option in Scotland abolished 1976
Norway	Company System or "Samlag" law introduced in 1871. Liquor stores run or controlled by local government, with a split of profits (65% to state, 15% to municipality, 10% to operators, 10% to public "counter attractions"). Also referred to as municipalisation or monopoly system. Similar to Swedish Gothenburg trust system. In 1894 the principle of local control enacted—local option gave a choice between prohibition or Samlag management. Scandinavian countries often focused on banning or taxing high alcohol content

(continued)

Table 2.1 (continued)

Country	*Local option prohibition laws on alcohol*
Canada	Canada Temperance Act 1864 allowed local option at the municipality or county level: by 1914, 520 Canadian localities banned alcohol sales. A referendum on national prohibition in Canada in 1898 saw a majority vote for prohibition but was not implemented as Quebec voted strongly against it. Some provinces voted dry in the early twentieth century: Prince Edward Island maintained prohibition from 1901 to 1948; and Ontario from 1916 to 1927. Canada also had federal prohibition over 1918–1920 as a war measure. Canada now has a government monopoly system in all states except Alberta. Exceptions apply for wineries and breweries. Prohibition in Ontario never really repealed, but instead gradually softened and modified. Some localities in Canada maintained dry status until the 1970s and, in The Junction area of Toronto, until 2000
New Zealand	Local Veto laws introduced in 1893. Areas could reduce or ban outlets with a 3/5th majority. Dry areas were "Dry Electorates" based on general electoral boundaries. Between 1894 and 1908, 12 out of 76 went dry. Polls held every 3 years to 1918. Examples of dry electorates: Clutha, Ashburton, and Mataura. In 1918 the local veto poll was abolished, but existing dry areas continued to vote. Later option included state purchase and control. Some areas were dry until 1999, and some liquor cooperatives created through local veto still exist. Liquor legislation still allows Local Alcohol Policies
Australia	Australian push for local option began from the 1860s, consolidating around Local Option Alliances following the 1880 Temperance Convention. States of New South Wales, Victoria, Queensland, South Australia, Western Australia, and Tasmania had some form of Local Option by the early twentieth century. For example, Western Australia referendum on local option 1911. Queensland introduced local veto in 1885. Canberra, the national capital, was founded as a prohibition city but overturned by popular vote in 1928. In recent decades locally defined dry areas controlling drinking in public spaces have become more common
(Victoria)	In Victoria 1870 legislation added the right of a municipality to object to liquor licenses based on existing license numbers. 1876 legislation froze licenses without a majority vote from electors (by municipality) to increase numbers. 1886 added a statutory limit of hotels per district. No licenses would be granted above the limit, and the number of licenses could be reduced or increased to the limit if a local option poll supported this. Considered unwieldy and inefficient: 168 polls but only 217 hotel closures 1906 legislation for a compulsory statewide local option poll in 1920. In the interim, the License Reduction Board closed 1317 hotels. The statewide local option poll held in 1920 required a 3/5th majority to close all hotels, or a simple majority to reduce license numbers. The poll created two dry zones, which remain in place in residual form today, and also resulted in around 200 further hotel closures. Dry zones have voted on all license applications subsequently, but the last statewide poll was held in 1938

> The experience of the United States of America, Canada, Norway, and Sweden, extended over many years, indicates that the power of local veto would be successfully exercised in many rural and suburban districts, and, possibly, in some small towns. (Rowntree and Sherwell 1899)

Typically a two-thirds or three-fifths majority was required to deny licenses or to vote an area “dry”. The definition of “local” or “area” varied but included subsets of electoral regions, liquor licensing districts, and less commonly (in Australia) was a function of local government. Different models proposed differing roles for direct democratic input and for government or judicial agencies. In some models, the majority opinion of voters was independent of any other authority, as in:

> If any village, town, or city, or any district of a town or city, wished to be without a public-house, it should be able by a popular vote to give effect to this wish, independently of any previous decision of the licensing authority. The majority required to give effect of the veto should, however in no case be less than two-thirds of those voting. (Rowntree and Sherwell 1899)

In other areas, including Victoria, local option combined direct democracy with bureaucratic decisions. In the United States, Local Option was sometimes referred to as Maine Law, based on the State of Maine which was first dry in 1851. Other US states followed including Kansas, Vermont, Iowa, and North and South Dakota. Oklahoma and Alabama enacted state prohibition in 1907, followed by Georgia. Local veto in the United States was valorised as ultimate democracy and criticised as ultimate despotism—highlighting contradictions and tensions inherent to local majority rule (Volk 2009), and around the places both of local rights and of alcohol in liberal democracies more generally.

The culmination of US counties, cities, and states voting dry over subsequent decades underscored the push for US national prohibition, later enacted through the 1919 Volstead Act. US national prohibition was repealed in 1933, but state- and local-level dry areas remained after this point. The repeal returned most powers around alcohol to local and state governments. Today 33 US states retain local option provisions for counties or localities to be dry by majority vote. Depending on source and definition, 200–500 counties or municipalities were still dry by local law in the United States in 2016. In Kansas, for example, counties were given the option to vote “wet” during the 1970s and 1980s, and a mix remains (Anderson et al. 2016). Over a quarter of Kentucky counties retain prohibition (Fernandez et al. 2018). A further 17 US states retain state monopoly controls on liquor sales. As the persistence of local dry areas demonstrates, a feature of the United States is its rights of municipal and state governments to self-rule (or "home rule").

Local option was first proposed in Britain in 1855. Although loosely based on Maine laws, Dingle (1980) notes key differences. Instead of being state level, proposed local option type laws in Britain were to be local (devolved) and permissive of local variation—hence legislation named the *Permissive Bill.* The first Permissive Bill was proposed in 1864. It was defeated, and revisited on seven occasions before morphing into the 1895 *Intoxicating Liquors Local Control Bill.* Apparently only by coincidence, Harcourt the small town in Victoria shared its name with Sir William Vernon Harcourt, the British Liberal Party politician and party leader who introduced the Permissive Bill to British Parliament on multiple occasions. The Permissive Bill hinged on local and municipalisation sentiment, but divided the Liberal Party between proponents of local democratic rights, and critics wary of the impact on individual liberties (Nicholls 2006; Nicholson 1990).

As did Liberals, British Socialists of the time argued both for and against local liquor controls, and the bill was never passed despite decades of lobbying. Only the Scottish equivalent passed. Scotland introduced local option provisions via the *Temperance (Scotland) Act* 1913, a success attributed to the strong influence of temperance and the Scottish Liberal Party (Kellas 1965). Dry areas in Scotland came and went—by 1970 there were 16 prohibition districts remaining. The system was abolished in 1976. Scotland also had and retains some Gothenburg or "trust" hotels. In addition, England and Scotland large landowners had often banned alcohol in their estates, as had some large companies, creating some private dry settlements.

New Zealand enacted local veto laws in 1893. A three-fifths majority of voters could reduce the numbers of licensed outlets, or ban outlets altogether. Voting areas were based on general electoral boundaries, and dry areas known as "Dry Electorates". Women were enfranchised early in New Zealand: in 1893, in a move tied to moral reform and the WCTU and also the influence of liberals like John Stuart Mill. The franchise was initially limited to ratepayers. Between 1894 and 1908, 12 out of 76 electorates in New Zealand voted dry. Results of these polls are mapped at Teara (2016). The overall proportion of "no license" vote in

New Zealand polls increased from 30 to 37% over 1894–1908. In 1918 the compulsory local veto system was abolished, but existing dry areas continued with the option to vote for prohibition, continuance, or for "state purchase and control". In 1945, amendments made the "dry" boundaries fixed and no longer aligned with electoral boundaries. Some dry areas existed until relatively recently—for example, Eden and Roskill until 1999. New Zealand retains liquor cooperatives and provisions for Local Alcohol Policies.

In Canada, the Canada Temperance Act 1864, or Dunkin Act, allowed local option at the municipality or county level. By 1914, 520 localities in Canada were dry—including most of Prince Edward Island. A referendum on national prohibition in Canada in 1898 saw a majority vote for prohibition. However, it was not implemented as the province of Quebec voted strongly against it and the central government was wary of dissent on the issue. Some Canadian provinces voted dry in the early twentieth century: Prince Edward Island maintained prohibition by referendum from 1901 to 1948; and Ontario from 1916 to 1927. Canada also had a federally ordered prohibition over 1918–1920, as a war measure, although this applied only to alcohol over 2.5% and exempted wineries and breweries. Canada now has a government monopoly system in all states except Alberta. Exceptions apply for wineries and breweries. Prohibition in Ontario was never specifically repealed, but gradually softened and modified, as detailed in Valverde (1998). Some localities in Canada maintained dry status until the 1970s and, in The Junction area of Toronto, until 2000.

Controls on alcohol in Scandinavian countries have characteristically been concerned with alcohol strength. They also have a tradition of local controls. The Company System—or "Samlag"—law was introduced in Norway in 1871. Samlag refers to liquor stores run or controlled by local government, with the profits returned to public institutions (specifically—65% to the State, 15% to the Municipality, 10% to operators and 10% to "objects of public utility, not chargeable to the rates, but operating as counter attractions to the public-house") (Snowden 1908, pp. 144–145). The system is also referred to as municipalisation as it allows alcohol, but captures the costs for local investment. Or it is referred to as monopoly system if no other alcohol outlets are allowed. In 1894 the principle of local control was enacted in Norway, giving a local option between prohibition, or Samlag management. Broadly similar arrangements existed in other Scandinavian countries including Denmark and Sweden, sometimes called the Gothenburg system.

The Gothenburg system created "trust" houses from which profits were directed to civic institutions such as libraries, museums, and parks.

An Australian push for local option began from the late 1860s, consolidating around the Local Option Alliances following the Temperance Convention of 1880. In 1866 in New South Wales, the Political Association for the Suppression of Intemperance demanded a "permissive liquor law" modelled on the UK Alliance's model. The Victorian Local Option Alliance was formed in 1882. New South Wales, Victoria, Queensland, South Australia, Western Australia, and Tasmania all had some form of local option by the early twentieth century. It was the flagship issue for temperance in Australia at this time. Queensland introduced a local veto system in 1885, and Western Australia held a referendum on local option in 1911. Victoria's first local option provisions came in 1870, escalated in 1876 and 1885, and culminated in a statewide poll in 1920. The spread of license limits, license reductions, vetos, and the dry zones created by local option in Victoria are examined in the next chapter. A feature of local option in Victoria was that the central government defined an acceptable "statutory limit" of densities of hotels per population, but that it was the decision of voters (until 1906 at least) whether or not to apply this ratio.

Motives for pursuing local-level temperance policies varied. While evangelical teetotallers may have set a total prohibitionist utopia in their sights, the emphasis on local option as a means to attain coincided with ascendant nineteenth-century values including classical liberalism, property rights, and municipalisation. Some campaigners sought an alcohol-free utopia and viewed local prohibitions as gradual steps towards total prohibition: (Nicholls 2006, p. 139; Lewis 1991, p. 53). Along these lines, Australian local option campaigners posed local-level answers to the rhetorical "drink question". Faith in the idea that change was not only possible, but practically inevitable, pervaded campaign material. The Australian Local Option Song, for example, called to:

> See the havoc drink is working,
> Everywhere the danger lurking;
> Shout, your duty never shirking,
> Alcohol shall fail!
> (Australian Local Option Song, quoted in Dunstan 1968, p. 102)

Similarly, in the lead-up to a local option vote in 1879, The Temperance Party urged locals to vote against license increases, and to see local option as part of a broader struggle for civic institutions and religious ideals:

> The struggle of the school, and the library and the church united against the beer house and the gin palace, is but one development of the war between heaven and hell. (*Camperdown Chronicle*, August 8, 1879)
>
> (Similar phrasing was also used in other temperance campaigns from 1868 onwards and cited in Lewis 1881, *The Drink Problem and Its Solution*, pp. 114–115)

Local option also stood as a proxy for voicing and opposing domestic violence: when in 1885 the Victorian Alliance for Local Option presented a petition by 45,000 women on a roll 1800 feet long to the Victorian Parliament, female petitioners called upon (male) parliamentarians to take note, among other things:

> That your petitioners regard the traffic in intoxicating liquors as at present exiting in this Colony, as the source of manifold evils to Society at large, and especially to many of their own sex, inasmuch as there are numerous women who are exposed to constant ill-usage, or who suffer equally cruel neglect, because those from whom they should receive protection are made brutal by intemperance. (1885 Local Option Alliance petition, quoted in Dunstan 1968, p. 104)

Liberal politics were also instrumental in pushing for local option laws, but for different rationales. In the classical liberal account, what was proposed was not a new control, but a change in its nature of power in a way better suited to the interests of competitive municipalities. UK Socialist party leader Snowden argued against State or total prohibition, arguing for local option independently on its own merits. To him and to key figures of the British Liberal Party, the option for local prohibition was an end itself: a means to move the costs of alcohol away from residential areas; to allow direct democratic participation in alcohol policy; or to return the profits from alcohol to community infrastructure. Snowden urged of local option in "Socialism and the Drink Question" that:

> To transfer the magistrates' power directly to the votes of the people is the assertion of no new claim by the community; it is simply a change in the

> method of exercising a right; it is a change from representative to democratic local government. (Snowden 1908, p. 120)

Dingle (1980) showed how support for local option grew from both sides of politics in England, as did opposition to it. Division within the ranks of temperance and local option campaigners also grew. Temperance groups in Australia were split on whether to focus on local option, or to settle for nothing short of total prohibition (Blocker et al. 2003, p. 77). Compensation was also a divisive issue. Volk (2009) argues that in the United States, while local option laws have tended to be remembered only as a minor part of broader prohibition politics, they also revealed:

> …a more complex mixture of both popular and elite participants struggling with whether majority rule and popular political empowerment always embodied democracy or freedom, or potentially their opposites. (p. 647)

Nonetheless, diverse temperance interests came together into alliances campaigning for these complex and sometimes contradictory powers. I examine the spread of and debates around local option laws, particularly as applied in Victoria, in more detail in the next chapter.

References

Anderson, D. M., Crost, B., & Rees, D. I. (2016). Wet laws, drinking establishments and violent crime. *The Economic Journal, 128*(611), 1333–1366.

Andrew, C., & Goldsmith, M. (1998). From local government to local governance—And beyond? *International Political Science Review, 19*(2), 101–117.

Atkinson, R. (2003). Domestication by cappuccino or a revenge on urban space? Control and empowerment in the management of public spaces. *Urban Studies, 40*(9), 1829–1843.

Bednar, J. (2008). *Robust federation: Principles of design (Political economy of institutions and decisions)*. Cambridge: Cambridge University Press.

Blocker, J. S, Fahey, D. M., & Tyrell, R. (2003). *Alcohol and temperance in modern history: An international encyclopedia*. Santa Barbara, CA: ABC-CLIO.

Booth, P. (2005). The nature of difference: Traditions of law and government and their effects on planning in Britain and France. In B. Sanyal (Ed.), *Comparative planning cultures* (pp. 259–284). London: Routledge.

Boudreau, J. A. (2003). Questioning the use of 'local democracy' as a discursive strategy for political mobilization in Los Angeles, Montreal and Toronto. *International Journal of Urban and Regional Research, 27*(4), 793–810.

Cadbury, D. (2011). *Chocolate wars: The 150-year rivalry between the world's greatest chocolate makers*. New York: Public Affairs.

Clarke, N., & Cochrane, A. (2013). Geographies and politics of localism: The localism of the United Kingdom's coalition government. *Political Geography, 34*, 10–23.

Dannenbaum, J. (1981). The origins of temperance activism and militancy among American women. *Journal of Social History, 15*(2), 235–252.

Davison, G., Dunstan, D., & McConville, C. (1985). *The outcasts of Melbourne: Essays in social history*. Sydney: Allen & Unwin.

DePastino, T. (2010). *Citizen hobo: How a century of homelessness shaped America*. Chicago and London: University of Chicago Press.

Dingle, A. E. (1980). *The campaign for prohibition in Victorian England: The United Kingdom Alliance, 1872–1895*. London: Taylor & Francis.

Dunstan, K. (1968). *Wowsers: Being an account of the prudery exhibited by certain outstanding men and women in such matters as drinking, smoking, prostitution, censorship and gambling*. Melbourne: Cassell Australia.

Facey, A. B. (1985). *A fortunate life*. London: Penguin UK.

Fernandez, J., Gohmann, S., & Pinkston, J. C. (2018). Breaking bad in Bourbon country: Does alcohol prohibition encourage methamphetamine production? *Southern Economic Journal, 84*(4), 1001–1023.

Fischel, W. A. (2004). An economic history of zoning and a cure for its exclusionary effects. *Urban Studies, 41*(2), 317–340.

Garnett, N. S. (2005), Relocating disorder. *Virginia Law Review, 91*(5), 1076–1112.

Gilling, T. (2016). *Grog: A bottled history of Australia's first 30 years*. Sydney: Hachette Australia.

Goebel, T. (1997). "A case of democratic contagion": Direct democracy in the American West, 1890–1920. *Pacific Historical Review, 66*(2), 213–230.

Herring, R., Berridge, V., & Thom, B. (2008). Binge drinking today: Learning lessons from the past. *Drugs: Education, Prevention and Policy, 15*(5), 475–486.

Hunt, T. (2010). *Building Jerusalem: The rise and fall of the Victorian city*. London: Hachette UK.

Isin, E. F. (2002). *Being political: Genealogies of citizenship*. Minneapolis, MN: University of Minnesota Press.

Jayne, M., Valentine, G., & Holloway, S. L. (2011). *Alcohol, drinking, drunkeness:(Dis) orderly spaces*. Aldershot: Ashgate Publishing.

Kellas, J. G. (1965). The Liberal Party in Scotland 1876–1895. *The Scottish Historical Review, 44*(137), 1–16.

Langton, M. (1993, March). Rum, seduction and death: 'Aboriginality' and alcohol. *Oceania, 63*(3), 195–206.

Lewis, D. (1881). *The drink problem and its solution*. London: National Temperance Publication Depot.

Lewis, M. (1991). *A rum state: Alcohol and state policy in Australia 1988–1988*. Canberra: Australian Government Publication Service.

Library of Congress Prints and Photographs Division. (1871). *Temperance illustration of drunkard hitting his wife*. http://www.pbs.org/kenburns/prohibition/popup/S0564/.

McComas, M. (2016). "Zoning" in on Maryland's nascent marijuana industry. *University of Baltimore Journal of Land and Development, 5*(2), 5.

McNamara, L., & Quilter, J. (2015). Public intoxication in NSW: The contours of criminalisation. *The Sydney Law Review, 37*, 1.

Merrett, D. T. (1979). The victorian licensing court 1906–68: A study of role and impact. *Australian Economic History Review, 19*(2), 123–150.

Mill, J. S. ([1861] 1989). *On liberty*. London: Walter Scott.

Németh, J., & Ross, E. (2014). Planning for marijuana: The cannabis conundrum. *Journal of the American Planning Association, 80*(1), 6–20.

Nicholls, J. Q. (2006). Liberties and licenses: Alcohol in liberal thought. *International Journal of Cultural Studies, 9*(2), 131–151.

Nicholls, J. (2011). *The politics of alcohol: A history of the drink question in England*. Oxford: Oxford University Press.

Nicholson, P. P. (1990). *The political philosophy of the British idealists: Selected studies*. Cambridge: Cambridge University Press.

Oldham, P. (2013). 'Suck more piss': How the confluence of key Melbourne-based audiences, musicians, and iconic scene spaces informed the Oz rock identity. *Perfect Beat, 14*(2), 120.

Pennay, A., & Room, R. (2012). Prohibiting public drinking in urban public spaces: A review of the evidence. *Drugs: Education, Prevention and Policy, 19*(2), 91–101.

Phillips, W. (1980). 'Six o'clock swill': The introduction of early closing of hotel bars in Australia. *Historical Studies, 95*(75), 250–266.

Pleck, E. (1989). Criminal approaches to family violence, 1640–1980. *Crime and Justice, 1989*, 19–57.

Pratchett, L. (2004). Local autonomy, local democracy and the 'new localism'. *Political Studies, 52*(2), 358–375.

Robbins, J. (1978). Localism and local government in South Australia. *Politics, 13*(1), 81–91.

Rowntree, J., & Sherwell, A. (1899). *The temperance problem and social reform* (6th ed.). London: Hoddor and Staughton.

Salkin, P. E., & Kansler, Z. (2010). Medical marijuana meets zoning: Can you grow, sell, and smoke that here? *Planning & Environmental Law, 62*(8), 3–8.

Silver, C. (1997). The racial origins of zoning in American cities. In M. R. Manning Thomas (Ed.), *Urban planning and the African American community: In the shadows*. Thousand Oaks: Sage.

Skov, S. J. (2009). Alcohol taxation policy in Australia: Public health imperatives for action. *The Medical Journal of Australia, 190*(8), 437–439.
Smith, J. K. (1982). An analysis of state regulations governing liquor store licensees. *The Journal of Law and Economics, 25*(2), 301–319.
Snowden, P. (1908). *Socialism and the drink question, The Socialist Library* (Vol. 6) London: Independent Labour Party.
Taylor, E. J., & Rowley, S. (2017). *Written in pencil or in ink: Private covenants and their legacies for housing and planning in Victoria*. Adelaide: State of Australian Cities (SOAC).
Teara. (2016). *Dry electorates.* http://www.teara.govt.nz/en/interactive/37611/dry-electorates, http://www.teara.govt.nz/en/diagram/37610/prohibition-referendums.
Tomes, N. (1978). A "torrent of abuse": Crimes of violence between working-class men and women in London, 1840–1875. *Journal of Social History, 11*(3), 328–345.
Ussher, B. (1985). The salvation war. *The Outcasts of Melbourne: Essays in Social History*. Sydney: Allen & Unwin.
Valverde, M. (1998). *Diseases of the will: Alcohol and the dilemmas of freedom*. Cambridge and New York: Cambridge University Press.
Volk, K. G. (2009). The perils of 'pure democracy': Minority rights, liquor politics, and popular sovereignty in Antebellum America. *Journal of the Early Republic, 29*(Winter), 641–679.
Weidenhoffer, M. (1967). *Garryowen's Melbourne: A selection from the chronicles of early Melbourne 1835 to 1852*. Melbourne, Australia: Thomson Nelson.
Williamson, A. P. (1992). Enterprise, industrial development and social planning: Quakers and the emergence of the textile industry in Ireland. *Planning Perspectives, 7*(3), 303–328.
Wright, C. (2014). *Beyond the ladies lounge: Australia's female publicans*. Melbourne: Melbourne University Press.

Newspaper Articles

"Suicide at the Porcupine", *Mount Alexander Mail*, Monday April 11, 1864, p. 3.
"A shocking wife murder", *Castlemaine Mail*, November 11, 1882, p. 4.
"*Local option in England*", South Australian Register, June 30, 1883.
"Macedon and Harcourt: Harcourt a voluntary temperance settlement", *The Bendigo Independent*, March 29, 1901, p. 3.

CHAPTER 3

The Live and Let Live Hotel, 1876–1912: Local Option in Victoria

Abstract In this chapter Taylor uses the example of the former Live and Let Live Hotel, in Barkers Creek, central Victoria, to track the effects of liquor licensing changes in Victoria during the period when anti-alcohol temperance alliances in several countries converged on calls for rights to local prohibitions on alcohol. The chapter analyses historical shifts in licensing legislation in Victoria from the 1860s to 1920s: early vetos, freezes on license numbers, voluntary polls, extensive hotel closures (including of the Live and Let Live) by the License Reduction Board, and culminating in the 1920 state-wide local option poll creating Melbourne's two "dry zones". The chapter newly maps the 1920 results, and corresponding Census data on religion. Taylor identifies legislative changes that increased local resident rights in licensing decisions, and argues these not only reshaped the hotel industry but helped establish planning norms around neighbourhood residential amenity.

Keywords Liquor licensing · Urban history · Temperance · Victoria · Historical GIS

The *Live and Let Live* was the stridently libertarian name of a hotel situated on Black Jack Gully Road in Barkers Creek, between Castlemaine and Harcourt in central Victoria. Licensed as a hotel for 36 years from 1876 to 1912, my father's maternal grandmother's family, the Luptons, were the licensees.

© The Author(s) 2019

E. J. Taylor, *Dry Zones*, https://doi.org/10.1007/978-981-13-2787-2_3

While the hotel was officially licensed from 1876, in earlier years John Lupton had appeared in court as one of numerous people accused of sly grog selling (unlicensed liquor sales) around the Mount Alexander goldfields ("Grog Selling: Castlemaine Court", *Mount Alexander Mail*, October 3, 1860). By the time his son James Lupton applied for a hotel liquor license in late 1875, the application was met with the early provisions of local controls on hotels in Victoria. A petition from local ratepayers sought to stop the license being granted, complaining the hotel was "not required", "would be a nuisance to the neighbourhood", and accusing what was then purportedly a grocery store of being "a 'low' house, a shanty…at which beer and liquor had been sold without a license". Edward Morton, licensee of nearby Morton's Hotel (see Fig. 1.1) also complained that the new license would threaten the viability of his own business.

Being a member of a well-connected Leeds commercial family may have subtly helped James Lupton's case. Otherwise, the fact he successfully obtained a license for the *Live and Let Live* can be attributed to luck with the views of members of the Castlemaine licensing bench on the day. Some of the bench questioned the new legislative provisions allowing the "requirement" for hotels in an area to be a consideration. From the bench, Mr. Merrifeld "thought the argument that a House was not required was a valueless one: if it applied to Houses in Castlemaine it might be said that many of them were not required". A lone voice of the three, Mr. Heron, was not in favour of Lupton and "said he thought the time had gone by for such houses but, as the majority of the Bench was against him, the license would be granted" ("Licensing Court—Applications", *Mount Alexander Mail*, December 13, 1875).

The *Live and Let Live* case reflects how, by 1875 a sentiment was increasingly expressed—by temperance campaigners, and within licensing laws—that there ought not to be so many hotels, and that the standard of hotels ought to be raised. The likes of the *Live and Let Live*—"such houses"—would no longer be encouraged, and especially not at great densities. Several decades later, in 1912, the *Live and Let Live* was closed by an agency, the License Reduction Board, set up to administer this view of hotels on a grand scale. Very shortly after the *Live and Let Live* was first licensed, in 1876, all new liquor licenses in Victoria were frozen pending a vote on local hotel numbers. For this and other reasons the *Live and Let Live* was the last hotel to obtain a license in the

Harcourt and Barkers Creek area. Its existence between 1876 and 1912 coincided roughly with the years of escalating local option controls in Victoria, through which it became harder to open new hotels and easier to close them.

Local option provisions, introduced in Victoria from as early as the 1860s onwards, gave areas opportunities to vote directly on local liquor licensing decisions or to limit licenses based on the existing number of hotels. This could mean reducing licenses (closures), or vetting new ones. Eventually there was the option to close all licenses. Few Victorian areas became fully dry, but many saw a significant reduction in numbers of hotels, and certainly a stalling of new ones. It was also through local option that parts of the state that were settled later in the nineteenth and early twentieth century—such as the Mallee and irrigation districts—came to have fewer, and by association larger, hotels.

Local option spread through the support of the temperance movement and through its appeal to other nineteenth-century ideals, including liberal democracy, in several countries (see previous chapters). This chapter tracks the emergence and influence of these controls in Victoria. It moves through early veto and local option provisions, the freeze on licenses and the introduction of a statutory limit on hotel densities, voluntary local polls, the License Reduction Board, and culminates in the 1920 statewide local option poll. It is based on historical liquor acts in Victoria published on legal database AUSTLII; combined with archival records (including government gazettes; digitised maps from the State Library of Victoria; and licensing records from the Public Records Office Victoria); secondary accounts (e.g. Dunstan 1968; Wright 2014); and historical GIS techniques.

The chapter identifies features of local licensing legislation during the temperance era that gave local areas rights to influence licensing policies and decisions. These helped establish legal norms of the neighbourhood: of amenity; quiet; and separation; and of who has rights to these and on what grounds. The chapter is structured around five phases:

- Local limits and vetos, 1865–1876;
- Freezes and triennial polls, 1876–1885;
- The statutory limit and voluntary polls, 1885–1906;
- The License Reduction Board, 1906–1920; and
- The Statewide local option poll, 1920.

3.1 Local Limits and Vetos

A first phase (1864–1876) of local alcohol controls in Victoria, *local limits and vetos*, saw the emergence of the idea of "sufficient" licenses, and an allowance for municipalities and neighbours to object to new liquor licenses in their area on this and other grounds including the "quiet of the place".

Since the establishment of the Colony in the 1830s and its split from New South Wales (1850s), Victoria always had a licensing system for alcohol sales, operated through a series of liquor licensing acts. Under these earlier Acts (1851, 1853), licensing applications and renewals were heard at annual licensing meetings, with decisions made based on retrospective information about licensee character and record. Under the 1853 Act if "a memorial in writing signed by five persons residing in the immediate vicinity of an house" held that a licensee "had been guilty of any abuse or infringement" then it was lawful for the licensing court justices to refuse an application. Thus, neighbours had some provision for objecting to existing licensed premises. In addition, in the Victorian Goldfields (including the Harcourt area), state-imposed prohibition had been in place from 1852 to 1854.

The first specific reference to a right to object to a new license based on prospective impacts seems to have come through the 1864 *Wines, Beers and Spirits Sale Act.* The Act contained provisions for the public to object to a license application if it was "in the immediate vicinity of" schools, places of worship (churches), or hospitals; or if the "the quiet of the place…will be disturbed". Where this idea of intrinsic neighbourhood amenity—broadly, civil institutions vulnerable to contagion (schools, places of worship, hospitals, quiet places)—came from is obscure, but it would go on to have a long legacy in Victoria. In the 1864 Act, objections based on the "quiet of the place" would be heard if supported by a petition from the majority of neighbours ("occupiers of houses"). Specifically, the 1864 Act allowed the following grounds for objection to be heard:

> That the applicant is of bad fame and character or of drunken habits or has within six months previously been deprived of a license or that the house in question has not the accommodation or is not of the materials required by this Act or is in the immediate vicinity of a place of public worship hospital or school and would if licensed be the cause of inconvenience or

annoyance to the persons using or frequenting such place or that the quiet of the place in which such house is situated will be disturbed if a license be granted for the sale of liquor therein. Provided that such last mentioned objection shall not be entertained unless a petition against the granting of such license be presented to such court of petty sessions signed by a majority of the occupiers of houses in the immediate neighbourhood of such house. (The Wines Beer and Spirit Sale Statute 1864, http://www.austlii.edu.au/au/legis/vic/hist_act/twbasss1864354)

This implied a role for a local majority to veto licenses ("signed by a majority of the occupiers") while also, implicitly, dampening the potential for vexatious objections by individuals. The concept specifically of *Local Option* was first proposed in Victoria in 1870, when George Higinbotham moved that two thirds of ratepayers in any borough should be able to vote against the granting or renewal of liquor licenses—that locals should be able "to say whether or not intoxicating drinks could be sold in their district". The proposal failed by a small margin. The 1870 *Wines, Beers and Spirits Sale Act* did, however, contain points of difference from preceding legislation on liquor licensing with regard to local property rights. Similarly to 1864, in 1870 permissible grounds for public objection were in part around the character of the licensee and their record; in part around meeting certain statutory requirements for accommodation at hotels; and in part related to what would now be termed residential amenity and separation (effectively, zoning)—"that the premises are in the immediate vicinity of a place of public worship hospital or school, or that the quiet of the place in which such premises are situated will be disturbed if a license be granted". In 1870, a right to object on such grounds were specifically named in terms of ratepayers not "occupiers of houses" as previously:

It shall be the right and privilege of any ratepayer in the district in which the premises proposed to be licensed are, or of any other applicant for a license or of any person already licensed in the district or of any member of the police force in charge of the district or place in which the proposed licensed premises are situated, or the owner or lessor thereof, to object at any licensing meeting or adjournment thereof to the granting renewal removal transfer or transmission of a license, and the objections that may be taken at the time of hearing such application may be one or more of the following:- That the applicant is of bad fame and character or of drunken habits, or has within six months previously been deprived

> of a license; or that the premises in question have not the accommodation required by the fourth section of this Statute, or reasonable accommodation if the said premise be not subject to the said statutory requirements or that the licensing thereof is not required in the neighbourhood, or that the premises are in the immediate vicinity of a place of public worship hospital or school, or that the quiet of the place in which such premises are situated will be disturbed if a license be granted, or any other objection (whether or not of the same kind as any of the preceding objections) which appears to the licensing magistrates to be sufficient. (s.11, The Wines Beer and Spirits Sale Statute 1864 Amendment Act 1870, Victoria, http://www.austlii.edu.au/au/legis/vic/hist_act/twbasss1864aa1870473/)

The 1870 Act allowed ratepayers (franchised property owners) to petition the court, and if it appeared to the magistrate that "a majority of the ratepayers" in the neighbourhood objected to a license then they were to refuse the proposal. The definition of a "neighbourhood" was as determined by the magistrates. The Act also added provision for a municipal body to object "on behalf of the ratepayers", to the granting of a liquor license where they felt there was already "a sufficient number" in the area of their authority. On this or other valid grounds, if it appeared to the magistrates that a majority of ratepayers in the neighbourhood objected, then they were to refuse the license. Specifically the 1870 Act allowed that:

> It shall be lawful for the council of any city or town, or of any borough or shire or the board of any road district to authorize any person on behalf of such council or board to object on behalf of the ratepayers of the same to the granting of an application for a license on the ground that there are already a sufficient number of licensed premises within the boundary's of such city town borough shire or road district, or in the part thereof in which the license of the said house is sought, or on any ground of objection mentioned in or authorized by the preceding section, and the licensing magistrates or such majority of them as aforesaid shall at the licensing meeting entertain any petition or memorial from the ratepayers of the said district on proof of the authenticity of the signatures thereto, and if it shall appear to such licensing magistrates that a majority of the ratepayers in the neighbourhood of the house proposed to be licensed object to the granting of such application, such licensing magistrates shall refuse to grant such application, and the licensing magistrate or the majority of them as hereinbefore mentioned shall in each case at their discretion determine

what is to be deemed "the neighbourhood" for the purpose of this section. (s.12, The Wines Beer and Spirits Sale Statute 1864 Amendment Act 1870, Victoria, http://www.austlii.edu.au/au/legis/vic/hist_act/twbasss1864aa1870473/)

This increased the direct input of locals—ratepayers, and local governments on behalf of ratepayers—in licensing decisions. Local ratepayer opposition had the potential to stop magistrates granting licenses if objectors to the license accounted for an apparent majority. Local authorities could also determine if the license were needed, with reference to existing numbers. The overall shift was tied up with property-based enfranchisement: with land ownership, settler colonialism, and with ideas of rights to quiet and of certain institutions to be kept separated.

These were the provisions that James Lupton encountered and narrowly evaded when seeking a hotel license for the hopefully named *Live and Let Live Hotel* in Barkers Creek in late 1875. Luckily for him, the petition of neighbours, complaint of another licensee, and claims there was no need for a hotel in the area did not carry obvious weight with decision-makers. Such rights to oppose hotels may, it could be inferred, have been partly symbolic. However they did represent an in-principle shift in rights between existing and proposed hotels, and between hotels and others.

3.2 Freezes and Triennial Polls

The 1876 licensing act in Victoria went further in setting the barriers to new hotel licenses, and in shifting the balance of rights in decisions in favour of residents. The 1876 Act froze all new licenses, without a majority vote from electors in a municipality to increase license numbers. It is generally (as in the License Reduction Board's later summary of the "Principles of Local Option under Various Systems in Victoria") considered the first application of local option in Victoria. Under the 1876 Act no new licenses were to be issued in any area (although it seems transfers were still possible)—until a poll of local ratepayers was taken that supported an increase. Specifically, although existing licenses at the time of the Act were not impacted:

> Thereafter no new publican's license except as aforesaid shall be granted in respect of premises situated in any municipal district or subdivision or in respect of premises situated in any ward of the city of Melbourne or town of Geelong unless and until the ratepayers of such municipal district or subdivision or the citizens or burgesses of such ward respectively shall have previously determined in manner hereinafter provided that the number of publicans' licenses for premises situated therein respectively may be increased by a given number. (s.18, The Licensing Act 1876, http://www.afstatuustlii.edu.au/au/legis/vic/hist_act/tla1876134/)

The system defaulted to a limit on new liquor licenses in an area, with provision for areas to vote to increase numbers. Plebiscites under this Act were triennial, with three held—1879, 1882, and 1885. The polls were referred to as "public house plebiscites", "licensing ballots", or "local option polls". They were undertaken alongside local government elections, and limited to (male) ratepayers. While based on *choice* the default setting mattered. Voters could vote *not to increase* the existing number of hotel licenses in the area, or to *increase* them—if the latter, they also had to specify the number by which. The slipperiness of this latter provision led to high rates of informal voting, and was a point of public confusion. *The Age* for example referred to doubt caused by "the obscure verbal collocation of Sections 22 and 23 of part 2 of the Licensing Act 1876" (*The Age*, August 13, 1879). In a letter to the editor in August 1879 (*Portland Guardian*, August 5, 1879), the 1876 Licensing Act was referred to "as is stands upon the Statute Book, a puzzle, which even the lawyers find difficult to unravel".

Notwithstanding local polls, the 1876 Act also allowed the Minister of Justice to designate special licensing districts where new licenses could be granted. This generally meant newly settled areas—at a time when the North West for example The Mallee area was being colonised. Becoming a special licensing district required petitioning the Minister and appealing to politically astute issues, as for example in the case of Dimboola in 1883, where supporters referred to a lack of hotel accommodation for railway customers.

There are no concise summaries of results of the triennial veto polls in this period. Of the reported results, the 1879 polls most often saw large majorities voting against license increases, with some areas recording significant numbers of informal votes. The requirement to specify a preferred number of additional licenses seems to have been especially baffling. In Eaglehawk, for example, some voters for an increase "outstepped the bounds of moderation, one wishing for an increase of 1000 while another individual declared in favour of an increase of 50,000" ("The Licensing Poll", *The Bendigo Advertiser*, August 15, 1879). Similarly, though less ambitiously, in Geelong West "two bibulous souls suggested that 100 new licenses be issued".

Some metropolitan results from the 1879 poll were reported in the *Weekly Times*, August 16, 1879 ("Council Elections and Licensing Plebiscite"); while *The Bendigo Advertiser* ("The Licensing Poll", August 15, 1879) reported some regional area results. Example results include Emerald Hill (now South Melbourne), with 1622 votes against an increase and 163 for; and Collingwood with 561 against and 8 for. Unusually, the Shire of Bellarine voted for an increase, favouring a new hotel in Queenscliff.

Next, the 1882 poll saw low voter turnout, but with most votes deciding against any increase in licenses. Some 1882 results were reported ("The Municipal Elections and Licensing Ballot", *Weekly Times*, August 12, 1882). Examples included Williamstown, with 119 for an increase in numbers and 296 against; and Footscray where "the few of the electors who voted were against any increase".

The polls themselves, under this system, seem to have had little systematic impact. The key impact for the purposes of this book is that the balance of rights between existing and potential liquor licensees, between licensees and local ratepayers, and between political and judicial powers, shifted further through the legislative changes of 1876. A new default setting—no new licenses—was established, and generally in favour of existing ratepayers. Legislation was complex and ambiguous, but overall presented new barriers to new liquor licenses, with new licenses only possible through political effort.

3.3 Voluntary Local Option Polls and the Statutory Limit

A next phase (1885–1906) in local liquor controls in Victoria was *local option and the statutory limit*. In 1885 local option legislation introduced a formal "statutory number"—an acceptable ratio of hotels to local population—and allowed locals to petition for a poll to either decrease or increase hotel numbers to this number.

Local option in Victoria came in earnest through The Licensing Act 1885 (amended in 1886, 1887, 1888, and 1890). The Act introduced a legislative "statutory number"—an acceptable ratio of hotels to the local population. This statutory limit added a measure through which hotel numbers could be not just limited, but bought down to standardised benchmarks. The statutory limit was 4 hotels for the first 1000 of population, and 1 hotel for each subsequent 500. It is not clear where this threshold came from. Locals could petition for a poll to either decrease or increase hotels to this number. The calculation of population on which the statutory ratio was based was based on multiplying the number of enrolled "rate paying electors" by a factor of five (presumably an average household size). Under the new system, licensing districts were based on Victorian Legislative Assembly electoral boundaries, rather than local government areas as in previous polls.

What the 1885 Act provided for was for locals—now defined as rate-paying electors (property-owning males)—to petition for a poll to either decrease or increase license numbers to the statutory number. If one-fifth of voters petitioned for a poll to be taken, voters could then determine whether to have more, or fewer, hotels (up to the limit, or down to the limit). A majority vote was required, and one-third of voters were required to vote for the result to be valid. Where the statutory limit had been exceeded, the number of existing licenses would be reduced to the statutory number if a local option petition and poll supported a reduction. Specifically:

> No new victualler's license shall be granted in any licensing district until the number of victuallers' licenses therein is reduced to a number below the statutory number of licensed victuallers for such licensing district nor unless the electors on the electoral rolls for the division of any electoral district forming the licensing district shall have determined in the manner hereinafter provided that the number of victuallers' licenses in such licensing district may be increased to a given number not exceeding the statutory number. (1885 Licensing Act, http://www.austlii.edu.au/au/legis/vic/hist_act/tla1885134/)

Hundreds of such voluntary polls were held in Victoria between 1886 and 1906. While overall hotel closures were considered small (217 closed, or a net of 57), there were significant closures in some areas including Geelong (1888) and North Melbourne (1902). In addition is the fact that no new licenses were allowed over the statutory number. Comparatively few areas successfully voted to increase hotel numbers *up to* the statutory number. Through the 1890 Licensing Act, irrigation districts had been excluded and placed under special restrictions—in the newly settled irrigation areas (Mildura and surrounds) no licenses other than grocer's, colonial wine licenses, or brewer's licenses could be applied for, and all licenses had to be with the consent of the Governor (s.176). Mildura did not obtain normal local option rights until 1916.

While the idea of voluntary local option polls had been of local self-determination: "to enable the voters in a licensing district to take the initiative with regard to the decrease or increase of licenses" (Licensing Court and Licenses Reduction Board—Fifteenth Report, 1922–1925), the License Reduction Board was later critical of the effectiveness (which it measured, naturally, in hotel closures). Later the LRB wrote critically that the net effect of 20 years of polls was "only 57 hotels": and also that "a considerable number of the polls taken, both for and against, were, through technical blunders, abortive".

If local option polls supported a reduction in license numbers in an area down to the statutory limit, the specific licenses to be deprived were decided by the Licensing Court. Their decisions were to take into consideration "the character and accommodation" of the premises; distances between premises; and an overall goal of retaining hotels that were "the best conducted" and which "afford[ed] the best accommodation". Compensation to licensees and owners was paid from a fund made up of license fees and fines. In addition, while the 1885 Act had a cap on new licenses, there were exceptions for very large establishments (with 30 or more bedrooms), and for roadside licenses. This could be seen as a first step in the establishment of much larger hotels and a much more concentrated industry structure. It coincided with the land boom and thus the elaborate multistorey hotels characteristic of the late 1880s, and was in tandem with the boom of equally giant and elaborate Coffee Palaces.

Wright (2014, p. 66) reports that in 1885 there had been 1046 hotels in Melbourne and 4299 in Victoria overall. Across the period 1885—1906, there were 168 local option polls held. Through this, 16 licensing districts successfully voted to decrease license numbers: this saw 217 hotels close. Meanwhile 60 districts successfully voted to increase license numbers: this (along with the provisions for very large and roadside licenses) saw 160 new hotels open. Hence, a net change of 57 hotel licenses in the state.

Applicants for new liquor licenses after 1885 also had to follow public notification processes, and licenses were sometimes conditional upon building to approved plans. Under the 1885 legislation, similar objection provisions as before were retained for determining individual license applications. It was the "right and privilege" of any three or more ratepayers to lodge an objection. There were also provisions for a simple direct veto on licenses without specific grounds—if a petition where "it appears to such licensing court that a majority of the ratepayers in the neighbourhood of the house proposed to be licensed object" were submitted, then license applications were refused by the court (Sections 70 and 71, 1885 Licensing Act http://www.austlii.edu.au/au/legis/vic/hist_act/tla1885134).

The net shift in hotel numbers in Victoria in the local option period, 1886–1906, was a decrease of 57 hotels. While hundreds of polls were held, many failed due to technicalities—particularly the requirement for at least a third of enrolled voters to vote. A key effect of the Act (as with 1876) is likely to have been a constraint on growth in hotel numbers, and a requirement that new hotels meet higher defined standards. Hotels holding licenses in 1885 would go on to have differing rights moving forward: later licensing records would sometimes mark "licensed since 1885" to denote this.

As to where the local option polls were held in Victoria, and the outcomes: the only consolidated information on local option polls in Victoria over 1885–1906 seems to be the License Reduction Board annual reports, which published an overview of the aggregate number of polls and closures under the earlier system. Individual closures under the voluntary local option system contain limited documentation. See for example Kennedy's Family Hotel in North Melbourne. This hotel was closed as a result of a successful 1902 poll. Pencilled annotation in LRB records only note "deprived 1904 or 1905?" The initial local option polls also met with several legal challenges around the validity of petitions and polls and the jurisdiction of the licensing courts to deprive licenses. Legislative amendments in later years clarified some points challenged in several of these cases, which had resulted in Supreme Court hearings.

In lieu of a more systematic source, the best information on local option polls and their results 1886–1906 seems to be searches of digitised newspapers on Trove, the National Library of Australia's online archive, combined with secondary accounts that refer to specific cases.

Secondary accounts such as local pub histories typically log all closures in a district in detail (but focusing on the later License Reduction Board phase). Histories of the temperance movement summarise aggregate rather than spatial data. Some of the local options polls mentioned on Trove, and the legal challenges to these polls, are summarised in the table in Chapter 7.

For example the Geelong North Poll, held in 1888, closed 18 hotels, but not before a Supreme Court hearing was required to "give effect to the determination of the electors". There had been 56 hotels in the district, with the statutory number only allowing for 16. Electors voted to close 18 hotels. Closed hotels in Geelong North included Dunn's Club and the Rising Sun in Ryrie-street; and the British and True Briton in Corio Street.

Castlemaine had a voluntary local option poll in 1888, for a district including portions of Campbell's Creek and Barker's Creek. A report from poll day noted "the proceedings were characterised by a good deal of enthusiasm on the part of both sides". Of 1069 eligible voters; 603 voted, and the vast majority for the continuance of the 51 existing hotels as compared to a statutory number of only 12. After the results, thanks were given by representatives of Castlemaine and Standard Breweries (*The Riverine Herald*, April 3, 1888), and "anti-optionists" sang celebratory chants. There were accusations that licensed victuallers from outside Castlemaine had organised the opposition to local reduction—a letter to the editor complained that "I think the excitement should be confined to the Castlemaine Borough…I fail to see what right other publicans have to interfere in the matter" (*Mount Alexander Mail*, March 27, 1888).

The effects of the North Melbourne (1902) poll are seemingly the best documented in this era. The poll voted on whether to reduce North Melbourne hotel numbers from 57 down to the statutory number of 20, thus closing 37 hotels. There were 1268 votes cast in total—sufficient to give effect to the reduction result. What followed was two years of dispute, largely in arbitration around which hotels were to be deprived of licenses (a decision made by the licensing courts), and how much compensation was to be awarded. The actual closures took place on May 23, 1905. The closed hotels in North Melbourne included the Rose of Australia on Courtney Street; Freemasons on Victoria Street; Kennedy's Family Hotel on Elizabeth Street; the Boundary on Boundary Road; and the Hit or Miss on Villiers Street. Temperance campaigners in North Melbourne, and beyond, were buoyed by the result. In a news report, one local option campaigner distanced himself from "prohibitionists" and emphasised the "vote of the people":

> Mr W.H. Webb presided, and said the people who had tried to reduce the temptations to drinking in the locality had been twitted with being prohibitionists, but they did not want prohibition unless by the vote of the people. ("North Melbourne Local Option", *The Age*, June 5, 1905)

This speech distanced state prohibition from local democratic control. Yet a different local option campaigner celebrating the North Melbourne result professed a *moral* opposition to hotels and objected to the compensation awarded to the deprived licensees. Recalling the fierce physical battles and rotten eggs hurled during the local option campaign:

> The Rev J.P. McCann, chairman of the local option committee, said he had an old coat at home covered with mud and stains of rotten eggs, and he intended to keep it as a relic of the local option campaign. The compensation paid was a dreadful piece of imposition, and he was sorry for the Government and the people, but was glad the hotels were closed. ("North Melbourne Local Option", *The Age*, June 5, 1905)

The North Melbourne Reverend resented even paying compensation to closed hotels, illustrating different views even on the same side of the local option battles. McConville (1984) also explored the impacts of North Melbourne pub closures on football cultures. Football, incidentally, was part of the public relations wars between temperance and hotel campaigners—temperance campaigners promoted sport as an alternative to drinking, whereas hotel keepers promoted their links to football teams as cultural value and as proof drinking could not be so ruinous to health as was claimed by temperance groups. Fierce confrontations—both physically, and in battles for public opinion—between temperance and hotel interest groups, and divisions within the ranks of local option campaigners, set the scene for the next phase of local option in Victoria—the License Reduction Board.

3.4 The License Reduction Board

The next, and the best already documented, phase of local option in Victoria came with the *License Reduction Board* (LRB) (1906–1920). A set of political compromises between the temperance movement and hotel industry produced the 1906 Licensing Act and the establishment of the LRB, which had a profound influence on hotel distributions on norms of liquor licensing in Victoria.

Merrett characterises the 1906 Licensing Act as a radical alteration to licensing laws in Victoria. It was intended to set the scene for statewide local option, but in so doing created a new level and structure of licensing regulation. The basic task of the LRB was to close "excess" licenses above the statutory number, by voluntary and involuntary means. The LRB also sought to increase both the size and standards of hotels (Wright 2014).

Over the period 1885–1906, license reductions had been undertaken by the Licensing Courts, empowered by local option polls. This earlier period had been characterised by a combination of judicial and democratic powers: a petition followed by direct votes determined whether or not local hotel numbers should reduce or increase, and the licensing court decided which individual hotels this decision would apply to. But this system came to be considered cumbersome and inefficient in reducing hotel numbers. The years 1906–1916 were to be very different.

Merrett (1979) describes the struggles between temperance and the hotel trade from the 1880s to 1906, and significant divisions within the two sides. Temperance proponents sought a stronger form of local option, but there were internal divisions over details such as compensation. The preferred version of local option from the temperance movement had no compensation. This jarred with more liberal proponents, and furthered stand-offs with the liquor industry. As both the temperance and hotel lobby weighed in on legislators, radical changes to local option emerged. Liquor interests—or the more influential among them—when given the choice between the vagaries of local democratic opinion, and the "standards raising" powers of a central board, preferred the latter. It was the moderate sides of both temperance and the liquor trade that created the LRB.

The legislative basis for this stage, the 1906 Licensing Act (http://www.austlii.edu.au/au/legis/vic/hist_act/la1906104/), also required a compulsory statewide local option poll to be held in the first general election after 1917. At this poll, all districts (217 electoral districts) in Victoria would be required to vote on licensing numbers—to continue license numbers, reduce them, or to cease all licenses via the "no license" option (total local prohibition). Crucially, the state poll would not be held for over a decade. In the interim, ahead of the poll, the LRB would bring licenses down.

The LRB was a centralised agency appointed by the state government and mandated to reduce hotel numbers down to the statutory limit for each licensing district. Hotels exceeding the statutory limit were considered "excess" hotels. Compensation for licensees was a core part of the Board's activities, with compensation paid from a fund raised via a 3% levy on liquor sales. License reductions could be voluntary (surrendered) or compulsory (deprived). Hearings took into account the size and financial viability of the hotels, with the Board explicitly targeting small operators and favouring larger, more profitable, and higher-class hotel operators (with encouragement from hotel lobby groups—Wright 2014, pp. 66–69). The LRB targeted what were considered the "worst elements" of hotels—small, dodgy, profligate operators.

The Board was initially set up to operate over 1906–1916, but the First World War saw its work extended until 1920. The LRB ultimately closed thousands of hotels in Victoria: Wright (2014) reports that by 1922 there were 2008 hotels left, a reduction of more than half since 1876 (pp. 68–69). There were two phases to this work. Most reductions were in the first 10 years when the Board closed hotels down to statutory limits by focussing on "overstocked" areas and "excess" hotels. Later closures in 1916–1920 were under a more general power to reduce district hotel numbers by up to 25%, while the LRB also took on licensing court powers.

In 1906, there were 217 licensing districts in Victoria containing 3523 hotels (including 75 roadside licenses). Of these, the Board found the statutory limit was exceeded in 120 districts, and thus confined delicensing activities over 1906–1916 to these areas. The Board closed 1054 Victorian hotels over the period 1906–1916, with former gold mining areas in and around Bendigo and Ballarat particularly impacted by the process. For example, between 1907 and 1920 the LRB closed 28% of Bendigo's hotels (54 of 302) and 28% of Ballarat's hotels (39 of 281) (Wright, p. 68).

The title of a history of pubs in Bendigo, "A Pub on Every Corner" (in several volumes) refers to the pre-LRB profligacy of hotels in that city (Houston 2009). LRB records for another former gold mining area, Ballarat West Licensing District, shows hotels with surrendered or deprived licenses are ruled out with red lines. In an example page of 32 hotels in 1906, 17 were closed during the 1906–1920 work of the LRB (PROV VPRS 7723 Hotel Licence Deprivation and Surrender Files).

Inner Melbourne areas including Collingwood and Port Melbourne were also heavily influenced by the LRB.

Under the 1906–1916 system the choice still remained for local districts to *increase* liquor license numbers for areas below the statutory imit. Petitions to hold a poll to increase numbers included Mimhamite (1907), Swan Hill (1909), Birchip (1909), Phillip Island (1910), Naracan (1911), and Otway (1913). Unsurprisingly given the hurdles and requirements involved, the number of new licenses granted in Victoria over 1906–1916 through this provision was very small relative to the number of closures: 33 new hotel licenses in total. Again this was associated with more recently settled towns having fewer but larger hotels.

Legislative changes in 1916 during the world war slightly expanded the LRB's activities, while also making the board permanent, and including the Licensing Court of Victoria in a statewide system. Through the 1916 Act, the statutory limit was abolished—instead, up to one-quarter of the existing number of hotels in any district could be closed. License limits were also refrozen to that of the existing numbers of hotels in the district as at 1st January 2017. Through these changes the Board "was empowered to proceed as if the Local Option provisions had gone into operation and 'reduction' had been carried in every district". In an extraordinary reversal of "local" and "option", the Board was free to reduce hotel numbers "where it was shown that a proportion could without public inconvenience be disposed with" (meaning, wherever the LRB felt like it). For an institution that measured its success in reduced hotel numbers, enhanced opportunities to close "redundant" hotels were appraised with glee:

> This was a most useful provision, and it enabled the Board to clear away many redundant hotels in old congested areas which previously could not be touched. (License Reduction Board fourteenth report, 1920–1922)

The provision for remote areas to petition to vote for an increase in license numbers was also changed in 1916, through the "Mallee" licensing option. The Board surmised that previously:

> Various unsuccessful mechanisms were made to provide workable machinery by which licenses could be got in newly developed or sparsely populated areas in the north, while at the same time preserving the unity of licensing districts in other respects.

The 1916 Mallee License provisions were introduced to allow the irrigated and newly colonised areas of Victoria to attain a hotel—subject to strict requirements on distance, and integrated with local option polls. This finally overrode, following some years of campaigning, the special temperance restrictions on Mildura and surrounds. After an area was proclaimed, an "inquiry and favourable report" was first required, followed by a majority local option result in favour of a license. This system prioritised Board assessments, but also made concessions to local option—the Board reported it "provides a number of useful safeguards, and satisfies local public opinion".

Through the Mallee Victuallers License provisions, 1916–1920 saw votes in favour of new licenses in remote areas including Manangatang, Ouyen, and Murrayville. The process also included the once infamously dry Mildura (which gained the Grand Hotel) and, later, neighbouring Merbein. Mildura had in the early twentieth century attained a small number of club and wine licenses, but no hotels or other license types until normal local option applied to the area. Mallee region hotels, most from the early twentieth century, are characteristically oversized—a 1924 news report noted how "big outlays in Mallee hotels have proved profitable" (*Geelong Advertiser*, July 16, 1924). The Mildura Working Man's Club had the distinction of having the longest bar in the Southern Hemisphere.

The total number of new hotel licenses issued in Victoria over 1916–1920 through this system was however, a mere 6. In the unlikely event of a liquor license being applied for, under the legislation objections to the grant or renewal of a license were also allowed by inspectors, councils, and "any ratepayer, freeholder or leaseholder of property situated within one mile from such premises".

What can be striking to a reader in the early twenty-first century is that the task of the LRB beforehand had been to close hundreds of hotels in Victoria in order to meet a statutory limit—bringing hotels per population *down* to levels remarkably *high* (1 for every 250 people) by today's standards. In 2016, Victoria had a Census population of around 6 million (5,926,624—ABS 2016 Census QuickStats). For the same year, Victorian Liquor and Gaming Commission data (VCGLR 2016) showed there were 20,293 liquor licenses in total in Victoria. Of these licenses, the majority (16,607) were restaurant and café licenses, producers' licenses, on-premises licenses (conference centres and etc.), packaged outlets, and minor limited licenses such as those for hotel mini-bars.

Excluding these categories—thus leaving general, club, and late night venues—there were 3683 licenses in Victoria in 2016.

The ratio of liquor licenses to population overall was 1 license per 292 people; and the ratio of more general hotel and club type licenses was 1 outlet per 1607 population. Even after liberalisation and considerable proliferation of cafes and social drinking, the current ratio is well below the statutory number as at 1885: a number that in many districts had previously greatly exceeded in the temperance era. It is worth noting at this point, however, that an estimated 80% of alcohol in Australia is now purchased pre-packaged (Livingston 2017). As a later chapter explores, concern about the impacts of alcohol has switched from hotels to a focus on large format packaged liquor outlets particularly in outer suburban areas (Livingston 2011; Morrison et al. 2016).

By 1920, ahead of the return to local option polls in Victoria, the License Reduction Board had established itself as a central, technocratic power largely divorced from local politics even if concessions were made to local consultation. The influence of the Board on hotel numbers in Victoria and, ultimately, the broader structure of liquor licensing and its regulation, was immense. The LRB had been a hugely successful, or hugely devastating (depending on your point of view), bureaucratic exercise, against which recent mourning of lost or threatened pubs in Melbourne (particularly those hosting live music—Homan 2011) pales in comparison.

3.5 The Statewide Local Option Poll, 1920

A fifth and final phase of local alcohol controls in Victoria in the temperance era was the return of democratic local option through statewide polls, with the first and most influential of these polls held in 1920.

Under the provisions of the 1906 and 1916 liquor legislation, the first statewide local option poll on liquor license numbers was held in 1920, following over a decade of LRB closures of hotels. Thus officially, the LRB's bureaucratic powers were returned to the democratic local option system at the point of the poll. The backdrop for the first Victorian statewide poll, and the first with the option of "no license" (dry) was that thousands of hotels had already been closed by the LRB, which had established itself as an authority on licensing standards. License numbers had been capped to existing levels for decades, and early (6 o'clock) closing had been in place for several years.

Merrett (1979) suggests the work of the LRB greatly reduced the democratic aspects of local option and the version preferred by temperance groups. By trimming what were seen as the "worst aspects" of liquor outlets, the reduction process meant temperance proponents lost ground to more moderate regulation. The temperance movement's political position was gradually diluted by the prominence of regulations appealing to normative idea of drinking standards. Altogether, the liquor licensing landscape had greatly changed between the peak of campaigning for local option, and the time of the statewide poll. So while prohibition seems "of" the 1920s, and national—probably by way of American imagery emphasising the 1919 Volstead Act—American national prohibition came at the tail end of decades of smaller scale prohibitions, and returned to these after repeal.

In 1920 there were 218 licensing districts in Victoria, based on electoral divisions. All enrolled voters (now including women) were allowed to vote on license numbers. The local option system required a 3/5th (60%) majority of district voters to return a no license (prohibition) result and thus close all liquor licenses in a district. A simple majority (50%) voting either reduction or no license was required to reduce license numbers to 3/4th of the existing number. Reductions were not confined to hotels and would include, for example, licensed grocers, although compensation was only provided to hotels.

Results of the October 1920 poll were published in the Victorian Government Gazette (November 19, 1920—see Chapter 7). Each licensing district was listed with the following information: district name, number on roll, continuance vote, reduction vote, no-license vote, informal, total votes polled, and returning officer's name. The overall result was 278,707 for continuation; 212,234 no license (40%); and 36,025 reduction. Two districts returned a "no license" result—Boroondara and Nunawading, both in Melbourne's east: these are the two dry zones remaining in residual form today 71 districts voted in the majority for reduction (that is, to reduce hotels by 25%). The remaining 144 districts voted for license continuances. The 1920 poll saw 107 hotel closures in total, across no license and reduction areas.

Historical GIS provides ways of presenting and interpreting historical events with a spatial dimension (for example Gordon 2011). To Orford et al. (2002), "mapping and spatially analysing historical data can often be crucial in understanding the patterns of present day social structures and the factors that have determined them" (p. 25). Using a historical GIS approach, I digitised and mapped the spatial dynamics of 1920 poll results. First I took the gazetted poll results from the Victoria Government Gazette, entered this into a spreadsheet, then calculated the percentage votes and checked these against the outcomes. I matched licensing district names and descriptions to historical maps and entered these into a GIS programme to attain approximate coordinates. I also matched results to 1921 Census data, on religious affiliation, at the local government level.

Similar challenges to historical GIS literature were true of this work as is described in historical GIS literature regarding recreating spatial records from qualitative sources (Orford et al. 2002; Gordon 2011). One basic technical issue was finding the details of licensing district locations. Victorian licensing districts in 1920 were based on electoral districts modified from the late nineteenth century. Maps of licensing district boundaries were not readily available. The approach I took to spatially visualising the data was to combine several different sources indicating where licensing districts used for the 1920 local option poll were located: 1900, 1913, and 1949 maps of state electoral boundaries (SLV 1900, 1913, 1949); a written description of electoral districts when they were announced in 1876 and when they were aligned to licensing districts in 1885; and licensing records which contained district names as well as hotel locations (PROV—VPRS 7723, 8159).

The 1913 state electoral map matched closest to liquor licensing district descriptions. The match of districts was to Electoral divisions of the Victorian Legislative Assembly. A small number of licensing districts in 1920 did not exist in earlier electoral maps; and vice versa. The 1913 electoral map also did not contain Melbourne metropolitan districts—only regional areas. For metropolitan Melbourne, similar 1900 and 1949 maps were used as reference points. While I cross-referenced between the different sources, the process involved potential error given few if any spatial representations of historical licensing data are available. I then digitised the 1900, 1913, and 1949 electoral maps in a GIS program by matching their features to recognisable points in aerial photography today; and created a GIS shapefile showing the location (the centroid point) of each licensing district. The spreadsheet of poll results by district was then joined to the constructed map file.

On average, districts voted 54.4% for continuance (wet), had only a small share of votes for the moderate option of reduction (6.5% on average), and returned a 45.2% no license (dry) vote. In the two dry districts, where over 60% voted for no license, 28.6% voted for continuance; and in the wet districts an average of 33.6% voted for "no license". Thus there were clearly patterns of difference between areas, but it is also noticeable how many voters in wet districts voted for no license or reduction—Hawthorn, Northcote, Brunswick, Moonee Ponds and Ballarat East had some of the largest numbers of no license votes but returned continuance as a percentage. This is partly because of a variation in district population sizes. On average Licensing Districts had around 4000 voters, however around 20 districts had over 10,000 voters on their rolls. Brunswick (25,240) and Northcote (17,648) were comparatively oversized licensing districts with significant temperance votes but returning wet results.

A graph of the spread of poll results is shown at Fig. 3.3, with the districts ranked from the highest percentage no license vote to the lowest. This graph also shows the total number of votes for no license in each district; the thresholds for a no license result (3/5th i.e. 60% majority no license); and for a reduction (50% no license or reduction vote). Brunswick had the single largest number of dry votes and was the largest district overall, returning wet (continuance) as a proportion (54.5%). Boroondara also had a large voter population, at 14,358, but with 62% of voters voting no license returned a dry (no license) result. As hoped for by liberal proponents of local option, local variations in views on licensing were reflected in differences in poll results. But areas—or least licensing districts—are not as homogenous in populations and views as the principles of local option (and local representation) would prefer.

The maps at Figs. 3.1 and 3.2 show the outcome of the 1920 poll for the Melbourne metropolitan area, and for Victoria as a whole. The continuance vote was generally stronger in the inner city of Melbourne; and the combined no license and reduction vote stronger in middle and outer suburbs. This included the east in particular where two dry zones resulted; but also the north-west such as Essendon.

The driest districts by percentage were: Boroondara, Nunawading, Malvern East, Warragul, Heywood, Kew, and Maldon. And by number were: Brunswick, Hawthorn, Boroondara, Northcote, Malvern East,

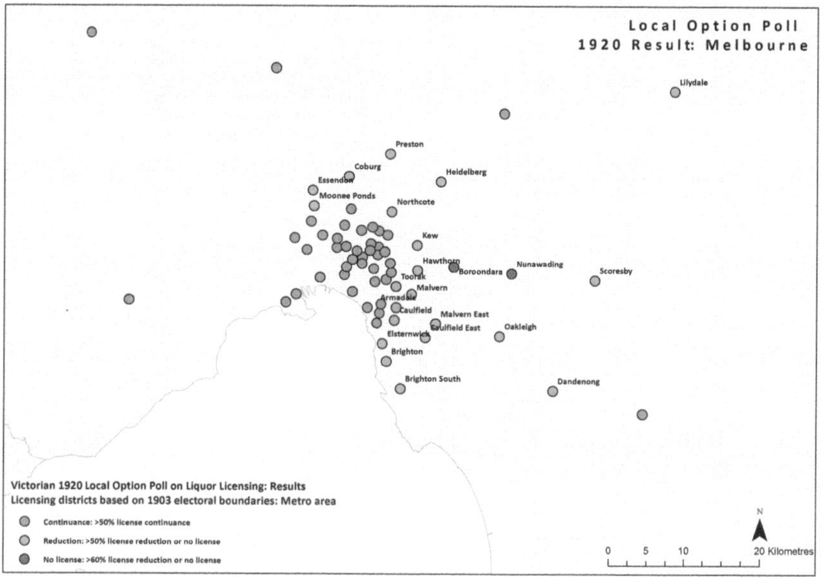

Fig. 3.1 Result of statewide local option poll—1920, Melbourne licensing districts

Caulfield East, and Ballarat West. The wettest voting areas by percentage were: Rutherglen (a long-time wine district); Chiltern, Warrenheip, Port Fairy, Lexton, and Bourke (in the Melbourne CBD). And by number the wettest areas were: Brunswick, Northcote, Hawthorn; Canterbury (in South Melbourne) and Footscray.

If the dry test had been for a simple majority of 50%, rather than 3/5th or 60%, then 25 Victorian districts would have been de-licensed—including Warragul, Malvern East, Maldon, Kew, Boort, and Lilydale. This threshold effect is shown in the graph in Fig. 3.3. Given the critical importance of where the majority line was drawn—simple, or three fifths—it is not surprising that the Victorian Local Option Alliance had in 1918 called for a simple majority. In Canada, for example, a 50% majority test had created hundreds of dry areas in addition to province-wide prohibitions.

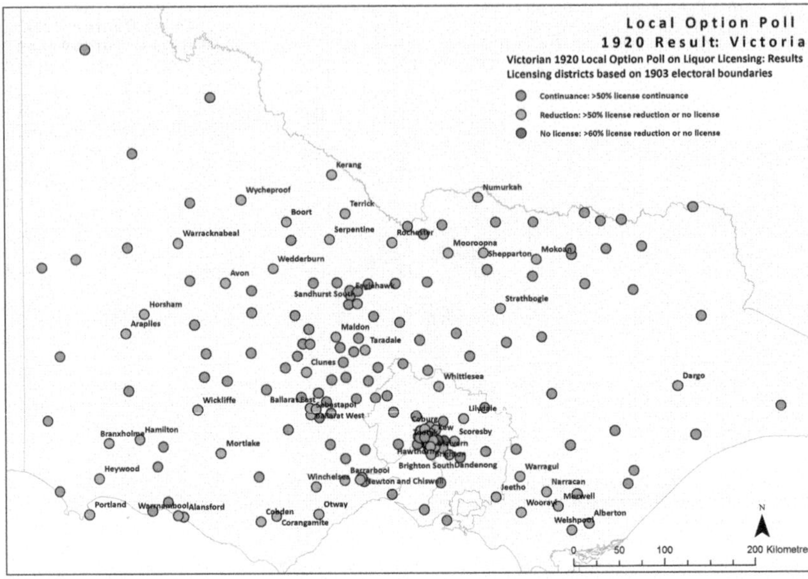

Fig. 3.2 Result of statewide local option poll—1920, Victorian licensing districts

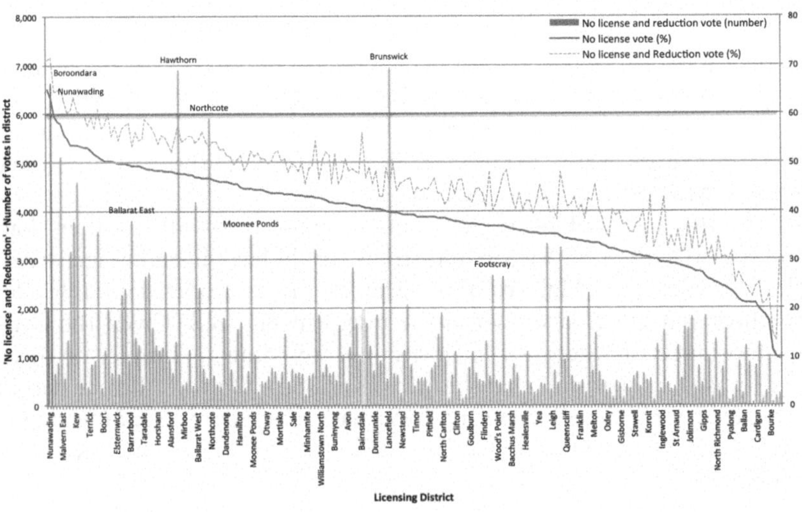

Fig. 3.3 1920 local option poll dry results by number, %, and threshold

3.6 Mapping 1920 Poll Results and Religion

To explore some possible explanations for spatial variations in the 1920 local option poll I matched the results to 1921 Census data (ABS 1921), at the local government area level. Historical census data are not published at other small area levels, so this is an imperfect approach. To map the Census results I entered the printed tabular data (religion by Local Government Area, by sex) into a spreadsheet and matched this list to a 1936 map (SLV 1936) showing cities, towns and boroughs of Victoria. Most 1921 local governments were represented in the 1936 map, however there were some small differences in boundaries between 1921 and 1930. For example, some boroughs separated from shires in the intervening period.

I undertook a concordance of the 1920 poll and 1921 Census files: between 217 Licensing Districts; and 194 Local government areas (comprising 55 Cities, Towns and Boroughs; and 139 Shires). Of these, 133 LGAs matched exactly to 1920 Licensing Districts by name or location. Other matches were many-to-one or one-to-many. In 38 cases there were multiple LGAs in a licensing district—most commonly 2 LGAs per district (for example the Town of Dunolly and the Shire of Bet Bet, both in the Licensing District of Dunolly). In these cases, LGA Census figures were aggregated to a Licensing District total.

More problematic were 69 cases where more than one licensing district fitted inside an LGA. In 14 of these cases, there were two Licensing Districts in one LGA. The more problematic cases were the LGAs of Bendigo, Collingwood, Essendon, Fitzroy, Malvern, and particularly Melbourne—each of which contained 4 or more licensing districts. The City of Fitzroy, for example, included Central Fitzroy, Clifton, North Fitzroy and South Fitzroy Licensing Districts. The City of Melbourne LGA (the innermost and densest part of Melbourne), contained 11 licensing districts. In these cases, the LGA Census figures were divided by the number of licensing districts to give each district an even share of Census counts. These cases unfortunately disguise what may have been smaller-scale variations in Census figures at a lower level.

The goal with the Census data was to consider the apparent relationships between demographic characteristics—focusing on religious affiliation—and local option poll results. Fernandez et al. (2018) found in Kentucky that religious affiliation predicted "dry", "wet" and "moist" areas. The Methodist religion is particularly associated with temperance politics (Bailey et al. 2007; Pegram 1997). Differences in poll results relating to sex ratios were suggested by newspapers at the time, as were concentrations of industries and social classes. While class and industry were no doubt relevant, the latter proved more difficult to digitise and recode, and are not covered here. The analysis here shows basic spatial differences in temperance votes, rather than undertake an in-depth statistical examination of results.

In the 1921 Census only 5810 (0.4%) of the Victorian population of 1,531,280 said they were not religious; and 9665 (0.6%) were of non-Christian religions. Rather than a newly religious or Christian influence, temperance politics more accurately reflected the influence of particular groups of Christian religions in a largely Christian settler nation. Within Christian affiliations, Methodists were primarily for temperance ideas and Catholics were primarily against it.

Religion partly reflected cultural and national differences—with Catholics in Australia often being of Irish or, later, Southern European descent and with different social norms around alcohol. The Methodist religion also represented particular views on the role of the individual—with a strong role for lay preachers, auto didacticism, and an emphasis on individual discipline and civic responsibilities (Bailey et al. 2007; Pegram 1997). As with protestant religions more generally in the nineteenth century, Methodists were associated with civic reform and an ethic of work. This is in contrast to religious ideals more focused on absolution in an afterlife and on formal hierarchical establishments. Methodists were also, like the Quaker abolitionists who also played a pivotal role in Temperance, influential in nineteenth-century commerce and industry, and so perhaps particularly well-suited to exerting political pressure. In Australia, amidst the fervour of patriotic support for anti-alcohol policies during wartime, Catholics were suspicious of being targeted by temperance laws (McKernan 1980, pp. 32–35).

The combined Census and licensing poll results show that on average, Catholics accounted for 21.7% of Victorian licensing district populations in 1920—this was far lower (8.9%) in the no license result districts; and was also lower in reduction districts (17.6%). Catholics accounted for a higher proportion of populations (23.8%) in wet (continuance) districts. There was a strong negative correlation between the no license and reduction vote at the licensing district level, and the share of Catholics in the population (a correlation of .599). This negative correlation is seen in the chart in Fig. 3.4. Conversely, and as expected, Methodist populations were positively correlated with the dry vote—accounting for higher proportion of population (16.7%) in no license districts; than in reduction districts (15.9%), or continuance districts (11.8%). There was

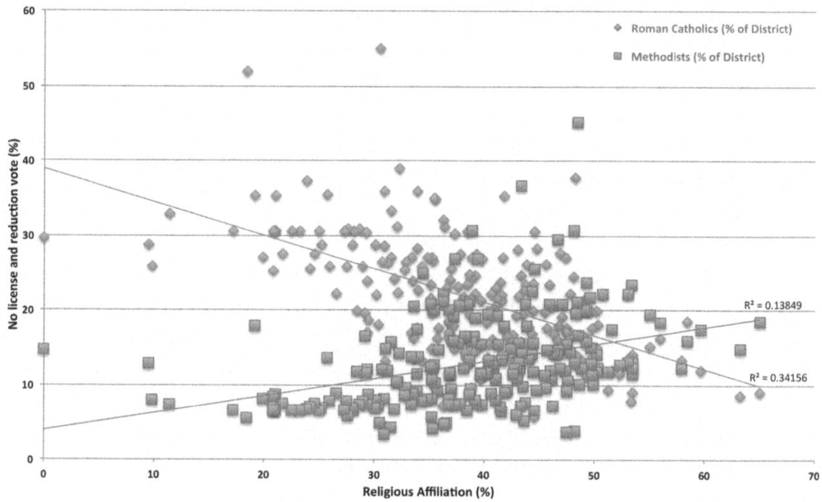

Fig. 3.4 Local option poll result—"no license" (dry) by Roman Catholics and Methodists (% of district)

a positive correlation (.319) between the Methodist population and the total dry (no license and reduction) vote of districts.

The largest populations of Methodists by percentage were Eaglehawk, Creswick, Sebastopol, Nhill, Clunes, Newstead and Fryers—all, with the exception of Nhill, former goldfields areas in central Victoria. The largest populations of Catholics by percentage were Koroit, Port Fairy, Bungaree, Allansford, and Pyalong—all, except Pyalong, being farming districts in western Victoria. Both religions (Catholic and Methodist) were in the minority—the Church of England was the dominant religion in most Victorian areas in 1920, and had no significant correlation with local option vote patterns. Whether a district voted in the majority for dry or continuance seems to have been less about the general population than the influence of more outlying religious groups with stronger views about temperance.

Voter turnout, which averaged 63.3%, was also higher in no license and reduction districts and positively correlated with the dry vote (.303) and with Methodism (.321): consistent with Methodists being more strongly engaged both with the local option cause, and with its democratic ideals. The average proportion of women (the sex ratio) was slightly higher in no license and reduction areas. Also of note was that people listing the Salvation Army as their religion in 1920 were a small group (only 9717 in total in Victoria), however that this group was most concentrated in Brunswick (505); followed by Prahran (380)—both strong wet areas by result. This is consistent, as per Valverde (1998) and others, with the idea that some Temperance-oriented groups took root in areas where drinking cultures were strongest.

Ultimately, details of how boundaries are drawn, and how a threshold is defined, can have long repercussions. The License Reduction Board record page for the Boroondara licensing district shows all hotels crossed out by the notation, "closed by local option poll" (PROV VPRS 7723—Hotel Licence Deprivation and Surrender Files). By the time of the 1920 poll, by various means, only one licensed hotel remained in Harcourt and Barkers Creek—the Old England Hotel. Given that the Taradale district (20% of it Methodist) voted for reduction, this last hotel too was to be closed. A news report noted that "the Taradale district has had more hotels closed in proportion to the original number than almost any other licensing district in the State". Half a century after the founding of the local IOR lodge, both Harcourt and Barkers Creek were, in effect if not name, fully dry (Fig. 3.5). In the town of Taradale, for whom the district was named, the last remaining hotel was also de-licensed in the 1920 poll.

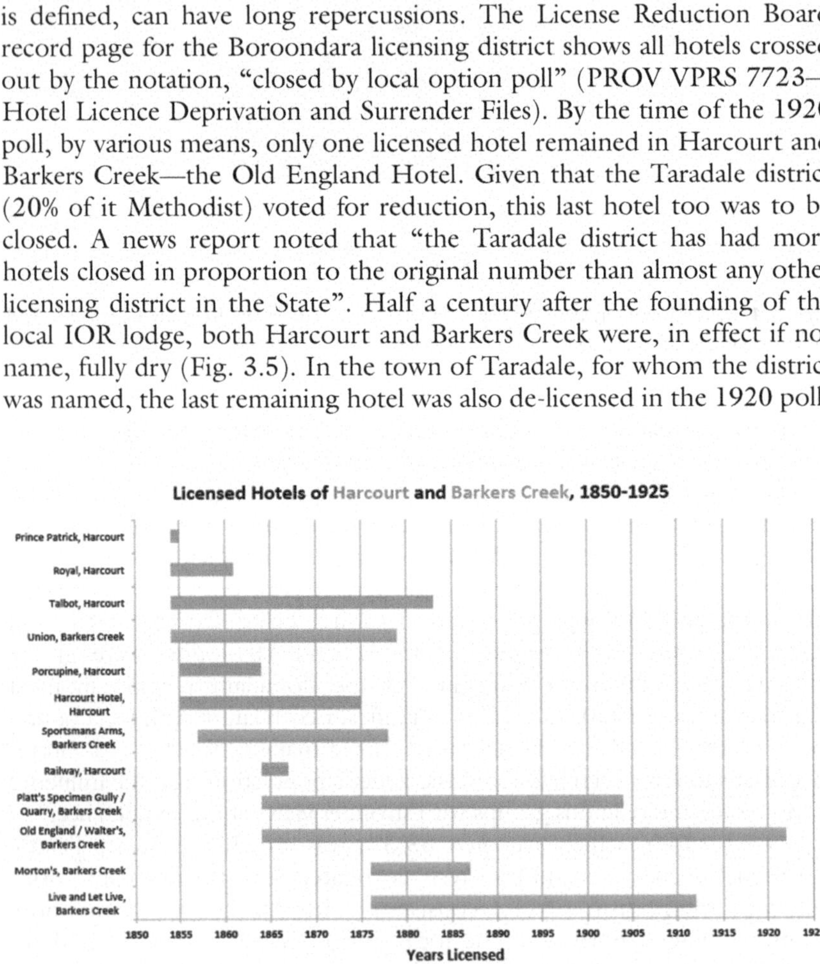

Fig. 3.5 Licensed years of hotels in Harcourt and Barkers Creek, Victoria

Meanwhile the *Live and Let Live* in Barkers Creek, which had scraped into a hotel license before local option legislation became more openly hostile both to new licenses and to smaller hotels in 1875, had been de-licensed ahead of the 1920 poll by the License Reduction Board in 1912. James Lupton died in 1912 after surrendering the license he had held since 1876. What was once the *Live and Let Live* is now marked by a plaque outside a bush-block home on the quiet, unsealed Black Jack Road.

References

Australian Bureau of Statistics (ABS). (1921). *Census of the Commonwealth of Australia 1921 part XI*. Victoria—Population of Local Government Areas, Cat. 2111.0.

Australian Bureau of Statistics (ABS). (2016). *2016 census quick stats—Victoria*.

Bailey, A. R., Harvey, D. C., & Brace, C. (2007). Disciplining youthful methodist bodies in nineteenth-century Cornwall. *Annals of the Association of American Geographers, 97*(1), 142–157.

Dunstan, K. (1968). *Wowsers. Being an account of the prudery exhibited by certain outstanding men and women in such matters as drinking, smoking, prostitution, censorship and gambling*. Stanmore, Australia: Cassell.

Fernandez, J., Gohmann, S., & Pinkston, J. C. (2018). Breaking bad in Bourbon Country: Does alcohol prohibition encourage methamphetamine production? *Southern Economic Journal, 84*(4), 1001–1023.

Gordon, C. (2011). Lost in space, or confessions of an accidental geographer. *International Journal of Humanities and Arts Computing, 5*(1), 1–22.

Homan, S. (2011). "I tote and I vote": Australian live music and cultural policy. *Arts Marketing: An International Journal, 1*(2), 96–107.

Houston, P. (2009). *A pub on every corner series: Bendigo & surrounds* (Vol. 2). Licenses Reduction Board 1910.

Licensing Court and Licences Reduction Board—Fifteenth Report, 1922–1925.

License Reduction Board—Fourteenth Report, 1920–1922.

Livingston, M. (2011). A longitudinal analysis of alcohol outlet density and domestic violence. *Addiction, 106*(5), 919–925.

Livingston, M. (2017). *Packaged liquor in Victoria: 2001 to 2016*. Canberra: Foundation for Alcohol Research and Education.

McConville, C. (1984). Football, liquor and gambling in the 1920s. *Sporting Traditions, 1*(1), 38–54.

McKernan, M. (1980). *The Australian people and the Great War*. Melbourne: Thomas Nelson.

McKernan, M. (1983). *All in!: Australia during the Second World War*. Melbourne: Nelson.

Merrett, D. T. (1979). The victorian licensing court 1906–68: A study of role and impact. *Australian Economic History Review, 19*(2), 123–150.
Morrison, C., Smith, K., Gruenewald, P. J., Ponicki, W. R., Lee, J. P. & Cameron, P. (2016). Relating off-premises alcohol outlet density to intentional and unintentional injuries. *Addiction,* 111, 56–64.
Orford, S., Dorling, D., Mitchell, R., Shaw, M., & Smith, G. D. (2002). Life and death of the people of London: A historical GIS of Charles Booth's inquiry. *Health & Place, 8*(1), 25–35.
Pegram, T. R. (1997). Temperance politics and regional political culture: The Anti-Saloon league in Maryland and the South, 1907–1915. *The Journal of Southern History, 63*(1), 57–90.
Public Records Office Victoria (PROV)—VPRS 7723 Hotel Licence Deprivation and Surrender Files, 8159.
State Library of Victoria (SLV). (1900). *Map of Victoria showing the twenty-three electorates for the Federal House of Representatives.* http://handle.slv.vic.gov.au/10381/120025.
State Library of Victoria (SLV). (1913). *Map of Victoria, 1913 [cartographic material]/photo-lithographed at the Department of Lands and Survey, Melbourne, by T.F. Mc.Gauran.* http://handle.slv.vic.gov.au/10381/120023.
State Library Victoria (SLV). (1936). *Railway map of Victoria [cartographic material]: Showing shires, boroughs, cities, towns and population.* http://handle.slv.vic.gov.au/10381/120026.
State Library Victoria (SLV). (1949). *1949 map of Victoria showing state electoral districts (urban and county).* http://handle.slv.vic.gov.au/10381/120010.
Valverde, M. (1998). *Diseases of the will: Alcohol and the dilemmas of freedom.* Cambridge and New York: Cambridge University Press.
Victorian Commission for Gambling and Liquor Regulation (VCGLR). (2016). *Liquor licences, gaming venues (VCGLR) 2016.* Accessed 23 June 2018 from AURIN Portal.
Wright, C. (2014). *Beyond the ladies lounge: Australia's female publicans.* Melbourne: Melbourne University Press.

Newspaper Articles

"Grog selling: Castlemaine police court". *Mount Alexander Mail*, October 3, 1860.
"Licensing court—Applications". *Mount Alexander Mail*, December 13, 1875.
The Age, August 13, 1879.
Portland Guardian, August 5, 1879.
"The licensing poll". *The Bendigo Advertiser*, August 15, 1879.
"The municipal elections and licensing ballot". *Weekly Times*, August 12, 1882.

"Local option". *Mount Alexander Mail*, March 27, 1888, p. 3. http://nla.gov.au/nla.news-article198933431.
"The local option movement". *The Riverine Herald*, April 3, 1888, p. 2. http://nla.gov.au/nla.news-article114659971.
"North Melbourne local option". *The Age*, June 5, 1905.
"New Underbool hotel". *Geelong Advertiser*, July 16, 1924, p. 6. http://nla.gov.au/nla.news-article166048345.

Australasian Legal Information Institute (AUSTLII)—Legal Records

Victorian Historic Acts:
Wines Beer and Spirit Sale Statute 1864. http://www.austlii.edu.au/au/legis/vic/hist_act/twbasss1864354.
Wines Beer and Spirits Sale Statute Amendment Act 1870. http://www.austlii.edu.au/au/legis/vic/hist_act/twbasss1864aa1870473/.
Licensing Act 1876. http://www.afstatuustlii.edu.au/au/legis/vic/hist_act/tla1876134/.
Licensing Act 1885. http://www.austlii.edu.au/au/legis/vic/hist_act/tla1885134/.
Licensing Act 1893. http://www.austlii.edu.au/cgi-bin/viewdb//au/legis/vic/hist_act/la1893104/.
Licensing Act 1906. http://www.austlii.edu.au/au/legis/vic/hist_act/la1906104/.
Licensing Act 1916. http://www.austlii.edu.au/cgi-bin/viewdb//au/legis/vic/hist_act/la1916104/.

CHAPTER 4

The Old England Hotel, 1922: Hangovers

Abstract Beginning with recent reports that Melbourne's two "dry zones" had been relegated to the history books, in this chapter Taylor proposes instead that contemporary urban planning continues to bear traces of the temperance movement of the late nineteenth and early twentieth centuries. These range from idiosyncratic dry zones and covenants; to ideas of residential amenity, separation and zoning; and objection rights of property owners. Taylor argues temperance ideas are still recognisable in the ways cities like Melbourne are organised. Characterising local option controls as a form of "planning before planning", the chapter critically examines how liquor licensing, zoning and metropolitan planning converged over the twentieth century in Victoria, reinforcing similar ideas around alcohol and land use and reshaping hotels into car and parking-oriented formats. Examples are given of planning conflicts—live music venues, packaged liquor outlets, fast food restaurants—with historical roots in local option politics of the temperance era.

Keywords Planning history · Liquor licensing · Zoning
Live music · Car parking · Australia

When Melbourne's two dry zones had compulsory ballots for restaurant and café liquor licenses removed in 2015, a news account surmised that "a hangover from the anti-alcohol movement of the 1920s had finally

© The Author(s) 2019

E. J. Taylor, *Dry Zones*, https://doi.org/10.1007/978-981-13-2787-2_4

been relegated to the history books" (*The Age*, May 13, 2015). As the preceding chapters described, the 1920 local option poll that first created these anachronistic alcohol-free pockets culminated half a century of campaigns in Australia and beyond for local-level alcohol controls. Yet the effects went well beyond the two no-license districts.

As one small example, in the same poll that created the Nunawading and Boroondara dry zones, the district of Taradale in central Victoria voted for license reduction. As a result, with few hotels actually left in the district, the *Old England Hotel* in Barker's Creek at which my maternal great-great-grandfather had (at least) once assaulted a publican with a fence paling, was de-licensed in 1922. This had been the last hotel in the Harcourt and Barkers Creek district. By that stage, through an accumulation of changes to liquor licensing, the district was dry in effect if not in name.

The Old England hotel building still stands today, and has been at times since a store, a museum, and is now a house (with the bar still inside, reportedly). Before researching this book, I had passed by the building many times with only mild curiosity. The Old England Hotel building and its setting have since shifted in my perception: no longer seeming only part of the inevitable fading of small goldfields settlements (some of which, in the 1980s and especially on Sundays, had seemed literally ghost towns); but as something also directly shaped by policies like local option. The Old England is one small piece of the physical legacy both of times of more profligate pubs in Victoria; and of the work of the statutory limit, local option and the License Reduction Board. There are similar signs to be found in other areas (Bendigo, Geelong, North Melbourne) where large numbers of hotel closures occurred in the late nineteenth and early twentieth centuries.

The preceding chapters of this book followed local liquor control in Victoria through the temperance era, from the mid-1800s and culminating in the 1920 statewide local option poll. Temperance ideas and proponents continued beyond that time (the WCTU still exists, for example), and the "era" is loosely defined, but its end is usually associated with the demise of national prohibition through the United States Volstead Act in 1933. This chapter focuses on the legacies today, for cities like Melbourne, of temperance era local liquor licensing politics. It is interested less in the facades of former hotels than in inherited traditions of the control of alcohol and land use. Dry zones might not be so easily relegated to the history books—they can also be read as chapters in longer, ongoing stories of how places are shaped by traditions of rights and controls. This chapter identifies ideas inherited from the temperance era by liquor licensing but also by systems of zoning and land use control.

In this chapter, I argue that contemporary land use control in Melbourne and other cities continue to bear traces of the temperance movement, and of the local controls that the temperance movement sought and partially achieved in the decades before planning was a formally defined bureaucracy. These range from Melbourne's idiosyncratic dry zones and anti-alcohol covenants; to more intrinsic ideas beyond specifically alcohol-related land uses—of residential amenity; norms of separation through the zoning out of literally and normatively polluting land uses; and the objection rights of residential property owners. The hangovers of temperance did not end either with the repeal of the Volstead Act or with, in Victoria, the end of 6 o'clock closing in the 1960s that marked the start of a process of licensing liberalisation. For one thing, land use zoning controls took up, duplicated, and have largely retained similar ideas around alcohol and land use and its place. For another, as the next chapter will examine in more detail, ideas resembling local option controls of the temperance era are now being reintroduced or newly strengthened, apparently for much the same reasons.

Valverde (1998) argued "liquor regulation strategies – with the exception of general prohibition – have been under-theorised even by those implementing them" (p. 146). Prohibition and dry zones can seem neatly or even humorously of the past, yet liquor licensing and planning regimes in the twenty-first century continue to control alcohol through what Valverde termed "many smaller prohibitions": layers of "street level" and "common sense" policies rarely subject to critical reflection (p. 148). Far from leaving wowsers behind, some temperance fundamentals are so intrinsic to the ways cities like Melbourne are run that it can take some reflecting to recall they have an inheritance at all, and have not simply always been that way.

4.1 The "Swill"

Through the combined work of the temperance movement, the License Reduction Board, local veto powers, and by nascent zoning and planning controls, the twentieth century in Victoria saw a vast suite of regulations established on sites for alcohol sale and consumption—on barmaids, room specifications, doors, toilets, bar positions, materials, fees, meals, the position of billiard tables, proximity to sensitive uses, opening and closing hours—whose full breadth it would be ambitious to even attempt to summarise. Of these the introduction and long survival of 6 o'clock closing is the most vivid and often told example. Early closing was introduced during the first world war, partly for patriotic reasons and partly to curb compromising incidents with troops. While intended to be temporary, it stayed in place to the mid-1960s in Victoria. Rather than a uniquely dated idea, early closing was the most tangible and extreme manifestation of liquor control, and can be understood as emblematic of a broader more complex regulatory regime.

One cited motive for early pub closing in Victoria was to encourage home life, and to discourage the later drinking temperance proponents linked to domestic violence. In practice, the introduction of early closing times is widely understood to have placed intense impact on the built form of Australian pubs, on industry structure, and drinking culture (Phillips 1980). An almost exclusively male clientele sought to drink as much as possible in the short hour available, conflating drinking alcohol with a swill not only of alcohol but of other bodily fluids. Oldham (2013) described "swill" era pubs as utilitarian and tiled, built for ease of hosing down. They were essentially entertainment-free and the domain of older men—"a social levelling, classless place which valued mateship and egalitarianism, and yet alienated women and younger male patrons" (p. 121). In a cynical account of 6 o'clock closing and its accompanying swill Dunstan (1968) grimly described the décor that resulted:

> Except for a few rare establishments seats were never provided, not even stools. There was no entertainment, except a radio droning out the races or football and the only decoration was the tiles on the wall, which enabled the bar to be washed down with greater ease after 6 p.m. If one needed a term to describe the decorative style it could be called Late Edwardian Urinal. (Dunstan 1968, p. 73)

As the hotel industry consolidated around established interests, drinking cultures consolidated around the swill. The swill characterised decades of general stasis in an industry of powerful but intricately regulated hotels. Lewis (1991) pointed to the perverse outcomes of early closing that proved hostile to the values that had promoted it:

> The temperance reform impulse, which advocated early closing in order to protect families, can be partially credited for creating drinking practices that were antithetical to civility, moderation and heterosociability. (Lewis 1991, p. 115)

Merrett (1979) critically summarised Victoria's licensing through much of the twentieth century. The driving logic behind regulations, he argued, was that *something* was under control—even though it is questionable whether this something was alcohol consumption or alcohol-related impacts. Although the system of regulation created large establishments with ostensibly higher standards and to avoid the excesses of hotel cultures past, Merrett argued they were ultimately of very low amenity and deterred new ideas.

To Johnson (2005) liquor licensing rules function more as narratives and warnings—about the place of women, for example—than as actual policies. In illustrating how such narratives influence the street level bureaucracy of liquor control, Valverde focused on post-prohibition Ontario (where prohibition ran 1916–1927). Licensing in the post-prohibition period in North America invented complex webs of street-level practices of regulation, all converged on avoiding a feared return of the "saloon". Bars in Ontario and British Columbia were forced to have fixed stools (p. 159)—a guard against leaning against a bar, a habit characteristic of the saloon. Styles of live music were subject to regular inspection for signs of saloon style sleaze. In post-prohibition western Canada food was banned, whereas to the same apparent purpose in parts of the US food was mandated. In British Columbia, beer parlours were allowed to sell "sandwiches"—but not "meals". None of this attention to furniture and food, Valverde observed, spoke directly to levels of consumption of alcohol. Indeed the net effect was often that:

> As long as patrons did not sing, dance, transgress the spatial boundaries assigned to them, or infringe the food regulations, they could drink all they wanted; and indeed the system assumed that the only valid reason for entering a beer parlour or tavern was to drink. (Valverde 1998, p. 160)

Although there were myriad small changes to details of regulating alcohol in Victoria in the decades following the first world war, essentially "the hotel industry was in stasis" (Lewis 1991, p. 48) until the late 1960s, and in some ways until the late 1980s. One further factor was that during the second world war resentment of American troops, and anxiety about drunken troops generally, fuelled sentiment against relaxed consumption of alcohol (McKernon 1983, pp. 201–204). The year 1956 saw a failed referendum for 10 o'clock closing in Victoria, partly in an attempt to cater for international visitors to the Melbourne Olympic

Games—in the end, Essendon Airport, on Commonwealth land, was one of the few available drinking venues at the games.

Real shifts in approaches to liquor licensing in Victoria began with a 1960 Act introducing restaurant licenses; followed by a 1963 Royal Commission suggesting drinking with food in relaxed circumstances was not harmful; and a 1966 report, the Phillips Inquiry, favouring liberalisation. The Victorian Temperance Alliance at that time changed its position on early closing, stating that early closing encouraged men to drink quickly and that "we have become convinced that our case was not solidly based, and that the only honest thing to do was to go before the Commissions and say so". The post-war decades also saw a slow resurgence of wine drinking in Australia and encouragement of the industry.

The 1965 Licensing Act added more licensing types, including for example theatres, to expand the social realm of drinking. Ten o'clock closing was introduced in 1966. The Liquor Control (Amendment) Act 1968 bought in more license types, extended drinking hours to 1 a.m., and reduced drinking age. This shift—and the need for hotels to adjust to new competition and preferences—signalled the beginning of the association of live music with licensed venues. Although a significant shift, the 1968 Act was still labyrinthine, and as Merrett points out, retained protection of existing liquor interests. For example, the 1968 Act contained requirements for retail liquor applications (supermarket bottle shops) to prove that "substantial demand exists" and "that substantial inconvenience results to the public in resorting to other existing licensed premises selling and supplying liquor" (s. 49)—not difficult to interpret as protecting existing outlets from competition. Further changes to liquor licensing occurred through the 1970s with the introduction of licenses for tourist facilities and "cider taverns". In 1983, a cap on ownership of 8% of all retail liquor licenses was introduced to slow the expanding dominance of major supermarket chains in packaged liquor sales.

The most significant reforms to Victorian liquor licensing laws came in the mid-1980s after the then Labor government appointed John Niewenhuysen, an economist from Melbourne University, to review the Liquor Control Act in 1984. The review resulted in a revised 1987 *Liquor Control Act*, which had significantly fewer licensing categories (reduced from 27 to 11), and allowed smaller licenses with lower entry costs and requirements. The reform principles were to seek "more civilised" drinking practices (Lewis 1991, p. 89), and to avoid protecting insider trade interests. In Nieuwenhuysen's account:

> The Act takes a cautious approach to added availability, not on economic protectionist grounds as in the 1968 Act, but on the basis of community interest...it shifts policy towards where it should be - finding means of containing abuse, rather than serving largely to protect those powerful trade interests, which have a habit of capturing liquor legislation in Victoria and elsewhere. (Nieuwenhuysen 1988, pp. 236)

Nieuwenhuysen characterised early closing as "a classic illustration of how circumscribing liquor laws can brutalize drinking habits" (p. 264). Referring to the problems with confining public drinking to public bars "perceived as male dominated spaces that are often too noisy and crowded, and to which people chiefly go to drink"; to Nieuwenhuysen the effects of "raised" standards in practice created "premises of a large scale nature, including the most notorious beer barns" (p. 270). The 1987 legislative changes to liquor licensing scaled back or removed many restrictions on obtaining a liquor license that could be traced directly to the temperance era. Its changes sought, in effect, the opposite of characteristic temperance era ideas: a greater number and variety of licensed venues, smaller venues, longer hours, and the hope that:

> New flexibility - especially to permit smaller scale, tavern like settings for drinking - may well be a substantial further move on the way to creating physical premises that permit a more civilized approach to alcohol consumption, and - perhaps - less abuse. (Niewenhuysen 1988, p. 270)

To some extent, hangovers from temperance history in Victoria could end on this point: the temperance era expunged by liberal reform. This is true in part: major changes were effected in Victoria, ahead of other Australian states. But it is not altogether so simple. The dry zones—and other restrictions on alcohol based on residential amenity—remain. Clues include the special licensing hours for ANZAC day, borne, like the 6 o'clock swill, of military anxieties of the early twentieth century. Licensed premises are highly regulated in Victoria within both the liquor licensing system, and the land use planning system that, over the twentieth century, emerged to duplicate many of the same controls that the temperance movement sought. Together these create "many smaller prohibitions" that continue to shape where and how alcohol is sold.

4.2 The Enduring Dry Zones

Perhaps the most surprising, or at least the most enduringly curious, hangover from temperance in Melbourne is the longevity of its two dry zones despite the demise of the local option system itself. After 1920, two further statewide local option polls were held in Victoria, in 1930 and 1938. Legislation in these later polls differed significantly. Controversial changes in 1922 legislation increased the size of licensing districts; moved poll dates back and further apart; reduced voter options; and shifted powers for license reduction to LRB discretion. Over the twentieth century, democratic local option and license reduction gradually receded and the Board and its successors became the primary power for liquor licensing decisions.

In 1922, the polls for 218 licensing districts in Victoria were replaced with polls for much larger aggregate areas—65 electoral districts. While under previous provisions the next statewide poll was to be held in 1923 and each 3 years thereafter, 1922 legislation pushed the next poll out to 1930 and then to every 8 years. Instead of 3 options for voters ("continuance", "reduction", "no license") the revised polls contained only 2 options—"continuance" or "abolition". Whereas previously a "reduction" vote would see hotel numbers reduced by 25%, under the 1922 legislation all discretion for reducing license numbers fell to the LRB. The Board could deprive licenses by up to 25% even in areas that had voted for license continuance. The 1922 changes thus represented a dramatically less "local" basis of control, and gave the central Board a broad brief to close hotels, specifically:

> Where the licensing court finds that the number of licenses of any description in any licensing district is greater than the number necessary for the convenience of the public or the requirements of a locality (but not otherwise) it may reduce such number in the manner provided in the Licensing Acts. (1922 Licensing Act, s. 31)

Temperance groups were frustrated with these changes, terming the new legislation "state option" as distinct from "local option". One article, "Local Option Poll: Postponement Resented", reported that campaigners from the Victorian Anti-Liquor League, and others contrasted state and local option in sharp terms. They:

> ...protested strongly against the action of the State Parliament in depriving the people of the long established right to deal with the liquor traffic by local option, and deplored the manifest insincerity of Parliament in passing an act granting State option in connection with the liquor trade. (*The Argus*, December 13, 1922)

For these and other broader reasons no new dry areas were created through the 1930 or 1938 polls. Nonetheless, campaigns for dry zones continued around both subsequent polls. For example, ahead of the 1930 Local option poll a Victorian Prohibition League poster showed clouds tracing out a shadowy word "Booze" over a pastoral scene, with a caption below "BOOZE: the shadow over our land: vote YES and remove it" (Victorian Prohibition League 1930). The poster visually combines place and property, with democratic rights; and is in contrast with other earlier imagery from the temperance era focused on the moral control of individual behaviour.

After the last poll, in 1938, restoration of the original local option process continued to be urged by Victoria's Local Option Alliance, calling for the government to "restore to the Statute Book local option as a fair and democratic method of liquor control" (*The Argus*, April 28, 1944). Local option was, however, deleted from Victoria's Licensing Act in 1946. While the revised Act in theory nullified the two dry zones (Boroondara and Nunawading), in practice this was far from accepted, and the fact that the dry zones resulted from popular votes had continued to carry particular bearing in public discussions. When an application for a hotel in Box Hill in the Nunawading dry zone was lodged in 1950, Local Option Alliance members emphasised at a public protest that:

> The vote of the people put the hotels out in 1920...there should be another vote before they are allowed to come back. (*The Age*, March 13, 1950)

Crucially, protesters against the Box Hill hotel application successfully made use of new *residential zoning* regulations ("Move to Oppose Hotel at Box Hill", *The Age*, April 21, 1950), and the hotel was blocked. This incident was followed in 1951 by petitions and protests against another proposed hotel in the Nunawading dry zone. Churches and other groups such as the Dry Area Defence League campaigned against the hotel specifically, and for the retention of dry status more generally. The local council passed a by-law preventing any liquor sales. Several years of dispute over the validity of this by-law followed, but ultimately the second Box Hill hotel proposal was also refused permission.

In 1953, petitions seeking to reinstate the local option polls signed by 5000 residents of dry areas were presented to Parliament as it debated liquor law changes ("Dry Area Might Get 'Reprieve'", *The Argus*, December 3, 1953). Under this pressure, politicians conceded that "elector's polls" would be held in the former dry areas created by the 1920 statewide local poll. Under the 1953 licensing Act, Victoria's two dry areas from the 1920 statewide poll attained their own special licensing provisions, as follows:

> Notwithstanding anything in the last preceding sub-section or in any other provision of the Licensing Acts where before the commencement of this Act a local option poll had been taken in any electoral district as constituted on the twenty-first day of October One thousand nine hundred and twenty and a resolution that no licenses be granted in that district had been carried.... (1953 Licensing Amendment Act, s7.3) http://www.austlii.edu.au/au/legis/vic/hist_act/la1953184/

Victoria's two dry zones have as a result voted directly on liquor license applications since 1953, having been fully dry between 1920 and 1946 and having fought off licenses by other means during the window 1946–1953. The 1953 and 1958 Licensing Acts, and accompanying Licensing Poll Rules (1965), set out the process for the "poll" or "vote" on applications to grant or renew in the dry areas. A vote was to be ordered for all electors "in the neighbourhood surrounding" the site of any license application. The delineation of a "neighbourhood" was as determined by the Licensing Court, after consultation with the Chief Electoral Officer. The legislation held that if the majority of electors in the defined neighbourhood voted against a liquor license, then the court would not grant the license, nor for 3 years afterwards. If the electors supported an application, then the court was not bound to approve it, but a majority refusal vote was binding.

The Licensing Act in 1968, although a considerable departure from established licensing law, continued the dry zone poll system. The 1987 legislation, representing an even more significant change to Victorian licensing legislation, also retained the dry zones. So too the 1998 Liquor Control Reform Act. This system has stayed largely in place to the present day. The Nunawading/Whitehorse dry zone was scaled back by vote in 1999, to exclude restaurant and café license applications from polls. And in 2015, the compulsory poll was removed (not by vote) for restaurant and café licenses in Boroondara: although it still stands for pubs, clubs and other license types in both. As the bulk of applications in the dry zones have been for café and restaurant licenses—essentially all of which had been approved in recent years—this change has been interpreted as the final demise of the dry zones. With the wind-back, a former Liberal Party State Premier observed in their defence that the "polls ensured the community had a say over neighbourhood amenity" and noted critically that Boroondara residents had not actually voted on scaling back the polls (*The Age*, May 16, 2015). Neither dry zone has any hotel, and only Nunawading has some club licenses.

In the United States, meanwhile, hundreds of dry counties and municipalities remain: for example in Kansas (Anderson et al. 2016); Kentucky (Fernandez et al. 2018); and 10 other states with local option or equivalents. In the United States postnational prohibition, some states maintained outright prohibition; some adopted licensing systems; and some introduced to state monopolies particularly over heavier alcoholic beverages. Today 17 US states maintain state monopolies or "alcoholic beverage control" (ABC) controls over heavier alcoholic drinks, although beer and wine are sold more widely. The end of national prohibition in the US technically meant simply that control of alcohol was returned to the states. State and local governments then continued to maintain local prohibition. The persistence of dry areas and of state controls on alcohol in Victoria as in the United States are reminders that systems of alcohol regulation are not binary—that while national prohibition ended, many smaller ones did not.

4.3 Local Option as Zoning (Before Zoning)

Other legacies from local option and the temperance era are less direct than the idiosyncratic dry zones, and are not confined to alcohol. The residential zoning and by-laws mentioned in the 1950 and 1951 Box Hill dry zone cases above are clues to this: in the temporary absence of the veto system, locals deployed other forms of control with the same effects as alcohol prohibition. Such by-laws and zoning controls continue, alongside liquor licensing systems, to shape where and how alcohol may be sold.

Two shifts in ideas about governing land use became clearer through the local option process: the licensed venue as a nuisance land use; and the matching inverse idea of a residential neighbourhood in which residents have the right to be pre-emptively shielded from such nuisances. Local option policies implicitly defined alcohol-related land uses as polluting; defined neighbourhoods in terms of residential amenity; and conferred residential property rights of objection against potential intrusions—including the idea that a larger number of objections had greater weight. These temperance ideas around alcohol are still recognisable today in expectations of separation and residential zoning; the rights of residential property owners to amenity and exclusion; the control of alcohol and other morally or environmentally polluting activities; and tensions around the role of direct democracy in policy. Some of these are intrinsic to the ways cities like Melbourne are organised, partly because temperance and the emergence of planning are closely linked in history.

For example, in debates about local option in Britain, Liberal politician William Vernon Harcourt compared liquor licensing to other early planning functions—which were at the time intrinsically functions of local government—public health, infrastructure, and sewerage:

> Matters affecting the public health, such as gas and water, were settled by persons representing individual localities, and as this was a question of morals as well a health and convenience it was not right to make it an exception. As restrictions had to be imposed locally, the question as to who should impose them was the only one of importance, and he had no hesitation in saying that it must be done by persons representing the sentiments of the community. (Sir William Harcourt summarised in *Local Option in England*, South Australian Register, Saturday June 30, 1883)

As anachronistic as dry zones are, it was actually through my research into contemporary planning conflicts in Victoria and the contested role of community objection and appeal rights within them (Taylor 2013, 2015; Taylor et al. 2016), that I first became interested in liquor licensing and its history. In the 2012 failed attempt of the residents of Tecoma, on Melbourne's hilly fringes, to stop a proposed McDonald's fast food restaurant, objectors used the statutory planning system to raise a concern common to many fast food opponents: antisocial behaviour. The planning tribunal (VCAT) established, however, that antisocial behaviour was not a valid concern. Alcohol would not be served, gambling not permitted, and no music or entertainment provided. Thus:

> We are not persuaded that a McDonald's restaurant is likely to lead to increased social problems in Tecoma. No alcohol is served in their premises. No gaming, music or entertainment occurs. (VCAT 2012 1539)

It struck me that this "common sense" observation might have made perfect legal sense; but that it was obviously discordant with what objecting locals actually feared as "social problems". The planning idea at work in the delineation of "antisocial" seemed to rely on older ideas and regulations applicable to the moral vices historically subject to outright bans or to control and licensing—alcohol, gambling, prostitution. I realised it was only around certain uses with these histories—including licensed venues, gaming machines and brothels—that social impacts were explicitly considered within the Victorian planning system.

Moreover, the Tecoma self-named "village" was not sufficiently *residential* to be afforded protection from any amenity impacts of fast food outlets. Had the McDonald's outlet served alcohol, or had the area been exclusively zoned residential, different thresholds would have applied. Again, seemingly common sense, but I wondered whether this revealed something about the legacies of history for planning disputes today. Further, while the number of objections received against the Tecoma McDonald's had no direct legal weight in the Victorian planning system at that time, there was a strong expectation that it ought to. A search for historical reasons for this lead to, among other places, the local option polls.

Drawing on the notion of genealogies of planning—of the nature of differences in traditions of planning rights and regulation (Booth 2002, 2005)—I came to the view that local option history has both legacies for, and parallels with, planning questions today. The temperance movement of the late nineteenth and early twentieth centuries made use of nascent planning law, specifically property rights and municipal corporations power. At a time when property owners and municipalities were ascendant, the temperance movement used emerging planning laws to legitimise the use of local popular political power, and to apply this power to the control of private liquor activity. This was only one part of a dispersed set of interests and motives involved in temperance political influence. But this process of setting local politics against alcohol is relevant to the emergence of zoning and land use controls, as it is to local politics today: how and why they arise, how they are debated, and the practical effects they can have. Much of what are pejoratively termed "NIMBY" disputes today sit at the edges of what is defined as polluting, and questions of who has the right to be separated from it.

Precursors to planning can be understood as escalating forms of control over urban space. A rough but overlapping trajectory runs from legal disputes based on the nuisance claims (Brenner 1974; Hamlin 1988; Meyer and Brown 1989); to local ordinances targeting nuisance from waste and animals (Atkins 2016; Brinkley and Vitiello 2013; Kiechle 2016); restrictions based on relocating immorality and disorder (Shumsky and Springer 1981; Garnett 2005); and to formal zoning to protect low density residential areas (Baar 1992; Dennis 1998, 2000; Fischel 2004; Jacobs and Paulsen 2009).

Key terms used in pre-planning conflicts were "nuisance" (meaning generally waste and animal-based pollution), and "evil" (meaning moral disorder). Meyer and Brown's (1989) survey of locational conflicts in nineteenth-century American cities emphasised the role of nuisance law as a common law legal precursor to public health regulations and to formal planning and zoning. Nuisance provisions, public health laws, private covenants, and liquor licensing predated but came to overlap with formal zoning and by-laws. Although not named as "planning", these all allocated and reallocated rights to space and to property, and were the focus of locational conflict.

What in the temperance era were conflicting new claims, are now institutionalised through land use zoning. The etymology of "zoning" is from a belt or girdle: deriving from classical symbols of moral containment—belts worn by Greek women to mark their status. Zoning spread rapidly in the early twentieth century, from Germany through other countries but especially the United States, as a means both to control unwanted uses and to protect residential areas. Zoning was a precursor to land use planning on a strategic or metropolitan level, and was preceded by similar dispersed mechanisms. Dennis (2000, p. 267) used the term "zoning before zoning" to describe growing legal and bureaucratic involvement in urban development over the late nineteenth and early twentieth centuries. The origins of planning controls in "zoning before zoning", and "before planning" are seen in private property law such as nuisance provisions, private property rights such as covenants, and the emergence of local corporations and municipalisation.

In response to industrialisation, public nuisance regulations on noxious trades were paired with rules from private citizens seeking to flee real and perceived invasions. Building on these proto-zoning beginnings, formal public zoning exploded in popularity across American cities in the early twentieth century. Claims of the need for domestic separation quickly spread from slaughterhouses and factories to include corner grocery shops, apartments, and classes and races of people. Racial zoning was an early feature, as were motives openly based on class prejudice and property values.

Hirt (2015) surveyed early planning traditions preceding and informing American zoning. Focusing on controls on private land, Hirt tracked traditions such as municipalities' and local laws; civil laws of trespass and nuisance; early building controls and codes; and private deeds (covenants). Early examples include by-laws confining noxious trades like soap making to outside of city walls. Both planning (or more directly, zoning) and local liquor controls emerged through similar forces—including real estate values and property rights; moralism; and (now largely discredited) public health concerns. Schilling and Linton (2005) observe that planning and public health have shared legal ancestors—that they "evolved from the same legal ancestors—the common law of public nuisance and the expansion of state police powers, both premised on protection of the public's health".

Victoria and Melbourne have their own peculiarities but are also broadly representative of other places with histories of colonialism; rapid growth from immigration; nineteenth-century industrialisation; an emphasis on freehold tenure and homeownership, and with formal zoning and planning from the early to mid-twentieth century. Processes of industrialisation and suburbanisation were, in Australia as elsewhere, intrinsically linked to the land tenure systems of colonialism, with land tenure what afforded early rights in determining local policies on alcohol, among others. Three basic elements to the emergence of local controls and zoning include:

- Controlling and zoning *out*: defining what is polluting.
- Excluding and zoning *in*: defining rights to residential amenity
- And within each: questions of who gets to decide and on what grounds.

As the next sections examine, liquor licensing and planning have converged on controlling alcohol-related land use across each of these elements.

4.4 Local Option and Residential Amenity

The 1920 local option poll that created Melbourne's two dry zones came as the culmination of half a century of campaigning for local option, and before Victoria had formal town planning legislation. Yet local liquor controls can be situated within the genealogy of planning: in the sense of traditions of law and governance legitimising culturally grounded controls and separations on the use of space (Booth 2002, 2005; Hirt 2015). Licensing control is one form of spatial ordering, one of several "traditions of law and governance" (Booth 2005) that used law to legitimise planning controls. Laws controlling public drinking and drunkenness were also amenity-based.

Nuisance provisions were deployed in industrialising nineteenth-century cities, but unevenly so. Nuisance claims in higher amenity residential areas had greater legal weight: lending gravitas to an expanding middle class to separate itself from industry and waste (Meyer and Brown 1989; Brenner 1974). Saloons were approached as nuisance uses in the nineteenth century. Nuisance ideas formed the groundwork for public health laws, which also emphasised separation often on the basis of now-discredited miasma theory of disease. While liquor licensing and local option have not been specifically examined from this point of view, Meyer and Brown's work highlighted the role of anti-saloon regulations in conflicts in Massachusetts cities. Meyer and Brown noted that "saloons viewed as 'noxious' facilities provoked far more conflict in urban America 100 years ago than they do now" (p. 108). They also noted how, in Massachusetts, the shift from illegal to regulated saloons saw more formal conflicts over alcohol—as regulation provides a forum for objection—and that Swedish neighbourhoods more consistently opposed new licenses.

A common thread to the emergence of public health, planning, and temperance was the principle of residential amenity. Anti-alcohol beliefs employed openly contagionist logic—for example the "modern plague of London" map, showing the distribution of public houses in London, published by the National Temperance Publication Depot over 1880–1885. Fischel (2004) argues that public zoning took over the function of private covenants, as a form of insurance for homeowners recast as public interest with a quasi-scientific basis. Booth (2002) also characterises a shift from private to public planning controls, noting that until the early twentieth century in England most "planning" was explicitly concerned with resolving disputes between neighbours and protecting private rights. Private property rationales for controlling land use only relatively recently morphed into public interest rationales.

The rise of local alcohol controls concurrent to ideals of suburban amenity can be interpreted as what Douglas (2003) and later Kristeva characterised as boundary making—with alcohol and its effects the waste that, by definition, is a product of trying to assert order (Moore 2012). Through the temperance era, liquor licensing came to overlap with early zoning and planning: which in Australia has, as in the United States, tended to put quiet residential amenity and the single detached dwelling at the pinnacle of uses to be protected (Hirt 2015). Whether endogenous or exogenous to actual drinking conditions, temperance ideas shaped an escalating expectation of separation of homes from drinking establishments, concurrent to ideals of a clean suburban home and its amenity value. These expectations were bolstered through the residential real estate market, with high-quality areas and homes sold with separation from alcohol as a feature.

Forms of local control—zoning and by-laws—were being adopted by some municipalities around the time of the 1920 Victorian local option poll, taking on a similar role to the private covenants already used—particularly from the 1880s—by developers of higher end residential estates; and by the use of civil nuisance grounds against various forms of pollution or invasion. Most by-laws and early zoning provisions related to protecting homes from intrusion—defining acceptable uses, densities, and materials. Thus the first decades of local option converged with local level zoning, with both serving to delineate acceptable locations for hotels, and standards of amenity for residential areas including separation and the setting of minimum standards for construction or lot sizes. In the Box Hill cases, when a local residential zoning by-law stopped the hotel, "the chairman of the bench…commented that the implications of the by-law seemed to be of major importance".

Although some local municipalities were already using zoning, in Melbourne, formal metropolitan level zoning was introduced through legislation in 1944 and the 1954 Metropolitan Planning Scheme. When metropolitan zoning controls came into place in Melbourne in the 1950s, zoning consistently separated hotels from homes, churches, schools, and hospitals. Zoning also reinforced a hierarchy of low-density homes above semi-detached housing and "flats" of differing scales and densities. Early anti-apartment concerns associating physical and moral degradation with housing other than single detached dwellings spread alongside zoning (Baar 1992). In Australia, the "flat evil" was a term used by the media to describe the first waves of local by-laws against higher density housing in the 1910s and 1920s. Much early regulation of land use was to minimise densities or to suppress the emergence of higher density housing in suburbs. O'Hanlon (2002) detailed the rise of local opposition to the "flat evil", with flats denounced as "anti-human, anti-family and un-Australian" (p. 126).

In the United States, early sporadic local laws against higher densities were strengthened with a Supreme Court ruling (Euclid v. Ambler 1926) establishing precedent for formal zoning to provide only "single family housing" to uphold "public health, safety, morals and general welfare" and avoid the imposition of a "parasitic" apartment building (Thomas and Ritzdorf 1997, p. 281). Euclid, and policies based on it, explicitly validated local rights to prohibit higher densities to protect low-density residential areas. Zoning as a precedent was exported to Australia (Freestone and Grubb 1998). Local building codes and by-laws also worked to minimise densities for several decades. From the 1980s onwards, successive metropolitan strategies to increase densities and housing mix have met with considerable angst—conflicting with an "embedded physical, institutional and cultural attachment to low-density urban form" (Hurley et al. 2017).

One lasting hangover of property rights and residential amenity and zoning ideas from the temperance era is the continued influence of temperance era restrictive covenants. Restrictive covenants illustrate one side of the emergence of local controls, and also their longevity. As restrictions bound to property titles, private deed restrictions, or covenants, have been a feature of property or land law in England and Wales since around the sixteenth century. They experienced a surge in popularity in the late eighteenth and early nineteenth centuries, associated with enclosure acts and with the emergence of exclusive private squares in response to industrialisation (Blandy 2006). Ironically, enclosures of the commons fuelled the migration that in turn, created the imperative to exclude.

In the late nineteenth and early twentieth centuries, before public zoning, private developers often introduced restrictive covenants to residential land sales. Fischel (2004) argues that public zoning took over the function of private covenants, as a form of insurance for homeowners later recast as public interest. Typical private covenants in temperance era Victoria stipulated building materials, limited building density and dwelling numbers, and prohibited the sale or manufacture of alcohol. Some were explicitly anti-alcohol and introduced by estate developers influential in the temperance movement. One example of alcohol-related covenants applies in a segment of Ascot Vale, a suburb in the north west of Melbourne, developed in 1886–1887 with covenants holding that:

> No building is to be erected on the land included in any purchase hereunder shall be used for a Brewery, Distillery, Public House or other place for the sale, storage or manufacture of spirituous or fermented liquor.

Covenants were also rapidly adopted in the United States through the late nineteenth century (Fogelson 2005; Fischel 2004; Hirt 2015). Propelled by developers catering to an emerging middle class, covenants emphasised strictly residential uses—pitched against the "nightmares" of mixed land uses, densities, and populations whose absence defined early suburbs. Migration from the south fuelled the demand to exclude, and covenants in the US context were often explicitly racial. When racial zoning (public policy with the same effect as a covenant) was found to be unconstitutional there was a surge in racial covenants, which were considered the exercise of a private right to exclude—an extension of rights to private property. Racial covenants in the United States were themselves later challenged on civil rights grounds. The 1949 decision did not invalidate racial covenants in themselves, but established that courts would no longer enforce them.

Although without explicitly racial content, in Australia's history private developers have introduced covenants to property titles. Typical private covenants stipulate building materials, limit dwelling numbers, and prohibit particular land uses or the sale of alcohol (Taylor and Rowley 2017). While some serve to protect business interests, covenants, like zoning, have tended to "put the single-family, owner-occupied home at the pinnacle of uses to be protected", and have functioned as security for homeowners and sale features for property developers (Fischel 2004). In recent legal decisions in Victoria, single-dwelling covenants, in particular, including those dating to the temperance era, have been upheld (VSC 2012). At the same time, they have an inherent conflict with housing and urban intensification policies (Taylor and Rowley 2017).

In 2012, failed bids for a liquor license and planning permit in the Victorian temperance seaside town of Ocean Grove, and a failed supreme court bid to remove the covenant, saw business closures in the town ("Bark Hut and Ti-Tree Village Holiday Park in Ocean Grove Forced to Close Because of Old Prohibition Law", *Herald Sun*, October 25, 2012). The temperance era covenant against alcohol sales, dating from the 1880s Methodist coffee palace resort development, was enforced until early 2014, when challenged by applicants for a liquor license. The administrative tribunal determined that although the Ocean Grove covenant was still legal, it was no longer enforceable due to a loophole identified in the original documentation—there were no longer identified beneficiaries to enforce the covenant clauses (*Geelong Advertiser*, March 13, 2014; Linaker v Greater Geelong CC [2014] VCAT 236). The covenant was varied to allow the restaurant to resume its liquor license. This mirrors changes internationally—the model town Bourneville recently obtained its first liquor license, actually an off-license for a newsagent just outside the covenant area, challenging to the late nineteenth century covenant (*The Guardian*, October 1, 2015). While these kinds of older covenants are being challenged, new forms of private zoning are rebounding, Deng (2003) argues that the more public planning promotes density and diversity, the more demand there is for exclusion of it.

Since 1864 in Victoria it was possible to object to liquor licenses if they were near to a place of worship, hospital, or school, or if they would disturb the quiet of the area. Objection rights around liquor licenses over time have mainly related to the separation of alcohol outlets from homes, quiet areas, and high-amenity moral type uses. There is a long tradition of certain civic and valued uses being kept separated from alcohol (see Chapter 7). Through these provisions, over the late nineteenth and early twentieth centuries liquor licensing legislation in Victoria came to integrate protections on local amenity including rights to object or veto license applications. Residential amenity and rights to object to developments seen to threaten it reflect ideas of the separation of housing, of low density housing in particular, but also of democratic rights. Property law has been central to this—local option votes were commonly, and in Victoria, based on the ratepayers. So too were rights to object to license proposals. The Victorian local government franchise (voting right) was explicitly based on property ownership and non-property owning residents were only franchised in local government in 1982.

The right to object to liquor licenses based on proximity to sensitive uses—schools, churches, quiet housing areas—shifted in small parts over time, but stayed essentially unchanged from 1864 until 1987. For example in 1928 legislation if "it appeared to the court that a majority of the ratepayers in the neighbourhood of the house" objected to the application, it was refused. After the arrival of zoning and then metropolitan planning, provisions for objection and petition rights against licensed premises were retained through the licensing system, and later doubled up through a parallel system for planning permissions. In 1965 liquor legislation, if 3 or more residents petitioned with 50 or more signatures, the LRB would define an area within which to assess local opinion about a license application. If after a month it appeared the majority of residents opposed the license, it was refused.

Under current planning and licensing legislation in Victoria, objections to licensed premises are possible through both systems—normally based on amenity (with respective legislative definitions) rather than the numbers of objections. However, the next chapter will show how calls for a more veto-based system are increasing and are being reintegrated.

4.5 Planning for Pubs, and Parking

Licensed premises in Victoria today are directly controlled by at least two sets of parallel regulation (Rowley 2017), each with provision for objections and protections on residential amenity—and each with requirements for car parking. Protections on residential amenity and, by association, influencing where alcohol may be sold or consumed have been institutionalised over the course of the twentieth century not only through liquor legislation, but also in planning, civil law, property law, environmental law, police powers, and local government by-laws. Council by-laws commonly ban consumption in public streets, and may ban or set defined drinking hours for the consumption of alcohol in public spaces such as parks.

When metropolitan zoning was introduced to Melbourne in 1954 (MMBW 1954), it formally separated hotels from residential zones in Melbourne. Under the planning scheme, a "hotel" meant "hotel licensed as such in accordance with the provisions of the Licensing Act 1958". Hotels could continue in place (via existing use rights), but not be granted new permission in residential areas. The zoning system also required off-street parking for new hotels: 1 space per 20 square feet of public bar; plus 1 for every 60 square feet of lounge or beer garden (MMBW 1959), or 1 space for every 1000 square feet for shops including the separate bottle shops which emerged from licensing changes in the 1960s. The distribution of older hotels in Melbourne today partly reflects the work of the LRB and local option polls, but also reflect the fact similar hotels could not be built in later decades, given their close proximity to residential areas and insufficient car parking. Zoning and liquor control instead produced fewer, larger, car-oriented hotels (sometimes called "beer barns").

Lower urban densities and land use separation were the focus of zoning policy for much of the twentieth century. Australian cities were developed under policy settings that celebrated the low-density house and garden suburban form; the sitting of industrial, commercial, and retail uses away from residential areas; and, after World War II, the prominence of the private car. The emphasis on residential separation, together with zoning features such as requiring car parking, goes no small way to explaining the built form of American and Australian suburbs. Zoning premises also helped create the separated big box packaged alcohol outlet that is now the focus of concerns about alcohol and place in Australian cities.

Victoria's liquor licensing legislation has explicit protections on local amenity—particularly residential amenity. While less code-based than preceding legislation, the 1987 reformed Act "based itself firmly on community interest" (Lewis 1991, p. 89). So too under the current *Liquor Control Reform Act* 1998. Any member of the community can object to a liquor license application on two main allowable grounds. One, impact on the *amenity* of the locality: that a license or licensing change would "detract from or be detrimental to the amenity of the area". And two—alcohol-related harm. Amenity under the *Liquor Control Reform Act* 1998 is defined as "the quality of an area that is pleasant and agreeable". Factors considered in defining amenity impact are parking facilities, traffic, noise, "the possibility of nuisance or vandalism", and "the harmony and coherence of the environment". The liquor licensing legislation seeks explicitly to "to contribute to minimising harm arising from the misuse and abuse of alcohol". After amenity, grounds for objection to licensing applications also include, for packaged liquor and late night outlets, grounds of *alcohol related harm*—that:

> Any person may object to the grant, variation or relocation of a packaged liquor license or late night (packaged liquor) license on the ground that the grant, variation or relocation would be conducive to or encourage the misuse or abuse of alcohol. (*Liquor Control Reform Act* 1998 38 (1A))

Under Section 76 of the Liquor Act the Victorian licensing authority is also required to take into account the "interest of the community", which "includes the interest of the community in protection of the amenity of the area". In so doing they take recommendations from local authorities and police, as well as community submissions. One change from liquor controls past is that community interest considerations now must not refer to affects on other businesses, or whether the business would be successful. This is in contrast to legislation from the 1960s and 1970s in particular which fairly openly sought to protect existing hotels from new competition.

New or expanding liquor outlets in Victoria need a liquor license, and all uses with a liquor license also have to apply for a planning permit under the *Planning and Environment Act 1987*. Today, under 52.27 (Licensed Premises) of the state standardised Victoria Planning Provisions, any new liquor license application under the *Liquor Control Reform Act* 1998 requires a planning permit. Additional hours or patron numbers also trigger planning permit assessment. Planning permit assessments are discretionary and, as in liquor license applications, consider possible amenity impacts and are open to public objection. Aspects of amenity considered relevant in the planning system in relation to licensed venues include parking, venue size, crowding, seating, food service, traffic, and hours. This closely, but not precisely, overlaps with considerations of the liquor licensing system.

Under the *Town and Country Planning Act* 1961 in Victoria, planning permits were required for most building works and, should a resident have objected to a council decision on a permit, there were appeal rights to the Planning Appeals Board. This board was established as a quasi-judicial body and has changed names several times. During a 1970s development boom in inner city areas, town planning decision and the appeals board came under scrutiny with calls for greater protection of heritage buildings, as well as provision for objections (Forge 1985, p. 15). Partly because of high profile cases, Victoria since established very broad rights of third-party objection and appeal around planning applications, with few limits on standing (Cook et al. 2012).

In Victoria now, *planning* permit assessments do not directly consider the possibility of nuisance or social harm from alcohol outlets. This is distinct from *liquor licensing* assessments, which do. Thus one set of legislation (planning) is principally concerned with amenity, and the other (liquor licensing) with social harm, but the two overlap to a significant extent. Both systems (liquor licensing and planning) consider car parking as a kind of amenity—with the view of providing more of it. Both the liquor and planning systems seek to protect local amenity; and contain provisions for local objections. The extent to which objections or popular opinion carry direct weight in either system has varied over the years but are under considerable pressure to again provide greater weight to local opposition.

Victoria's liquor licensing has been liberalised in the sense that smaller bars, particularly in established commercial areas, are much more easily licensed now than in the twentieth century. However, the valorisation of residential separation and particularly of low-density housing that characterised early temperance and zoning movements remains a central concern of planning systems. Hotels and other licensed venues are zoned out of residential areas; and additional protections and vetos on amenity are in place for residential areas in both the liquor licensing and planning permit processes.

Other uses have similar grounds for separation or objection: in the case of brothels in Victoria, similar locational restrictions apply as the grounds for objection to liquor licenses in the mid-nineteenth century—brothels (under planning law and the *Sex Work Act 1994*), cannot be close to a home, place of worship, hospital, or school. Similar rules also apply to sex shops (shops selling pornography). A move from criminalised to licensed and zoned activity occurred around prostitution (legalised in Victoria in the 1980s); and is underway in American states and Canadian provinces where forms of cannabis sales are being legalised (McComas 2016; Németh and Ross 2014). Planning approaches are tending to treat cannabis outlets like bars or sex shops: preventing their density, limiting their location near schools churches or residential areas, with "local jurisdictions…applying the same proximity buffers used to separate sex-oriented businesses from residential areas and sensitive uses such as schools, parks, and playgrounds", also "employing density controls commonly used to control bar and liquor store density, most often the spacing between such facilities" (Németh and Ross 2014).

Ultimately, while liberalised in the abstract, in space and place, there are still sharper divides around alcohol and around other land use issues. In the Tecoma McDonald's case, the Tecoma was not sufficiently residential to be afforded protection from the amenity impacts of fast food outlets (Taylor 2015). Had the McDonald's served alcohol, different thresholds of impact would have applied. Had the area been zoned residential, as in a similar case immediately preceding the Tecoma one and where the restaurant was refused planning permission on grounds of residential amenity, different thresholds would again have applied. Meanwhile, most existing hotels and bottle shops in inner Melbourne exist through existing use rights and would be difficult to legally build now in such proximity to dwellings and with limited onsite car parking.

Objectors in the 2012 Tecoma McDonald's case indicated an expectation that residential areas would have a level of veto rights to exclude certain kinds of activity. Their expectations that this would cover an unlicensed fast food restaurant, in a small "village", and that the number of objections would directly count against the proposal were not true of the Victorian planning system at the time. However veto rights against licensed premises, in more strictly residential areas, and with provision for majority vetos (petitions or votes), have long histories and, as the next chapter will discuss, are being reasserted.

4.6 Music and Big Boxes, Smaller Prohibitions

The layers of control on modern liquor licensing in Australia can be illustrated by looking at issues around live music venues, and by the emergence of big box packaged liquor outlets. In Australia, backlash against the effects on live music of increasingly strict licensing laws (themselves prompted by concerns about violence) are a focus of public debate, including the "Save Live Music" rally in 2012. An interest in how to protect and foster live music, and how to respond to conflict around it, is a theme in Australian planning research (Burke and Schmidt 2009, 2013; Homan 2011; Shaw 2005). Recent decades planning policies have sought to protect live music in inner areas, while acknowledging some of the amenity challenges involved.

Over a similar time period, but in different locations, planning research, and policies have started to discourage the size and proliferation of "big box" packaged alcohol stores in suburban areas. Both issues—the closure of music venues through noise complaints, and concerns over large packaged alcohol stores—illustrate some of the legacies of temperance before planning, and the layers of control on alcohol. Each in a sense are managed by, and created by, regulatory changes.

Liquor licensing changes seeded the "pub rock" movement and the now embedded links between live music and liquor licensing. Previously, the live music scene, at least in Melbourne, had been centred on all-ages venues that did not serve alcohol (Oldham 2013). In the wake of 1968 changes (longer hours, lower drinking age, more licensing categories), some hotels began to cater to live music and entertainment. Today, the fate of Australian live music venues is all but inseparable from liquor licensing. Political activities to save live music have often focused on iconic individual hotel venues.

As a result of concerns that planning approvals for new housing were worsening noise complaints and putting pressure on licensed venues, in 2014 "agent of change" rules were introduced to the Victoria Planning Provisions (52.43) "to ensure that the primary responsibility for noise attenuation rests with the agent of change". A noticeable feature of "agent of change" principles in planning is that they do not extend to the environmental protection, criminal, and liquor licensing legislation under which noise complaints and rights actually operate. They are planning rules relating only to changes in use and development. In the planning system, existing uses have long enjoyed existing use rights at the property level—an existing legal use can continue indefinitely after zoning changes. The critical issue in live music is that existing use rights do not extend to causing nuisance (such as noise pollution). Liquor licenses by contrast are personal rights attached to particular licensees and places and can be withdrawn. The enforcement of conditions and hence the survival of hotels in residential areas can, depending on specifics, involve councils, police, courts, or the Environmental Protection Agency.

Thus Agent of Change provisions introduced in Victoria in response to disputes over music noise from licensed venues demonstrate the complex ways in which liquor licensing and planning systems overlap. In the planning system, there are two competing impulses—supporting music and the night-time economy, and controlling impacts from alcohol including amenity but more recently a focus on violence. When planners seek to "plan" for live music, live music debates show historical legal differences in the rights afforded by different sets of legislation, each of which are products of history and converge on issues of urban space in a largely uncoordinated way. The parallel existence of rights across liquor licenses, planning permits, and environmental protection illustrate their shared roots in nuisance law, and in early suburbanisation. Such layers of smaller prohibitions are not so easily expunged. In Brisbane, Burke and Schmidt (2009, 2013) argue that planners may want to plan for live music, but the extent of overlapping regulation is often beyond their powers. There are also unintended consequences: in Brisbane, zoning approaches to live music have had successes in retaining venues but also created monopolies in regulated businesses and emergent unregulated venues.

The Agent of Change laws also serve to further lock-in historical patterns of uses and rights: protecting existing licensed venues, and existing residential areas, but preventing new venues in residential areas. The main use of the provisions has been to pre-emptively stop apartments near a music venue on a nineteenth-century shopping strip (Mylonas v Darebin CC [2016] VCAT 1583, September 19, 2016). Although there is no evidence of who objects to live music—whether they live in new apartments, or existing homes, the changes effectively curtail the rights of new apartment builders and developers but not those of existing residents. Paying disproportionate regulatory attention to new apartments has, of course, a long zoning tradition behind it.

Regulatory hangovers extend from music venues in inner Melbourne, to big box outlets in outer suburban areas. Concerns about the proliferation of large format bottle shops and their links to domestic violence were central to Victoria's *Hunt Club* case (Hunt Club Commercial Pty Ltd v Casey CC, VCAT 2013), in which the local council and community representatives wanted to restrict a large format bottle shop on the grounds of cumulative social impacts including domestic violence. A planning tribunal rejected the concerns, and granted a planning permit. The *Hunt Club* finding did not necessarily assert that bottle shop density would not cause social impacts, rather that social impacts such as domestic violence were not relevant planning considerations. Testament to the complexity of smaller prohibitions on alcohol, the applicants subsequently had to obtain a *liquor license* and followed an overlapping process of objection and debate around amenity impacts within a parallel yet slightly ajar system.

The physical form of this contentious new bottle shop was also a reflection of twentieth-century zoning: separated land uses, with ample car parking prioritised (Shoup 2005). Bottle shops have their own branch of liquor licensing history in Victoria. Prior to the 1950s, single-ownership licensed grocers were the standard outlet for bottled alcohol in Victoria. A rise in separate bottle shops, and more recently big box formats, has been in part facilitated by minimum parking requirements and expectations of separation for new developments. Corporate ownership of liquor stores was constrained in Victoria between 1983 and 2000, with caps on the share of ownership (to 8% of the total retail liquor outlets) by individuals or corporations. Changes to ownership laws in 2000 removing caps on shares of ownership have seen a new proliferation of corporately owned big box liquor stores often in outer suburban locations.

Since the removal of restrictions in ownership in 1998, major supermarket chains have expanded ownership into an emerging oligopoly of liquor outlets in Victoria. Woolworths purchased the five-chain Dan Murphy's store in 1998, expanding to 66 stores in 2018. Coles (owned by Wesfarmers) owns Liquorland, with 84 stores, and other major outlets. Livingston (2017) found there were 2023 packaged liquor outlets in Victoria, with 14.5% owned by Woolworths; 10.7% by Wesfarmers; and 6.3% by ALDI; plus 37.3% "operating under one of the Metcash brands". Around a third were independent outlets. The number of packaged outlets increased by half between 2001 and 2016, ahead of population growth. Around 80% of alcohol in Australia is now sold in packaged format. Victoria's rise in big-box supermarket-owned liquor stores has occurred through specific changes to legislation and is not shared in all Australian states—in Queensland, for example, supermarket liquor sales are banned; and in the Northern Territory liquor store floor sizes are capped.

In Sydney in 2013, a news report "Community rejects bottle shop by school" (*Sydney Morning Herald*, August 4, 2013) detailed how a chain bottle shop had been rejected by a council on the back of local opposition, citing research linking alcohol availability and domestic violence. Proponents of the bottle shop rejected the decision as "quasi-prohibition". Although contested, such density measures have clear historical parallels in statutory limits and the license reduction board and to temperance campaign interests in alcohol as an aggravator of domestic violence. Despite the effort to distance planning from liquor-related social harms as in the *Hunt Club* decision, planning, and alcohol policy remain interlinked in complex ways, with overlapping roles for community objection and for differing measures of community impact. Each value stories of containment, which like the temperance logic that informed them, are rife with unintended consequences—good, bad, and occasionally baffling.

Hotels are doubly regulated spaces, of which requirements for car parking are emblematic. In a not dissimilar way to car parking, in Victoria, liquor licensing requirements meant hotels were early adopters in requirements for sanitation and toilets. Hotels had requirements as early as 1890 for baths and toilets, and before that for adequate facilities by the standards of the time—although Melbourne was not connected to a sewerage system until 1902. The Sportsman's Arms in Barkers temporarily lost its license in 1861 for being dirty and "not within the requirements of the Act". In a 1936 case in the town of Kyneton, the town itself had no requirements for sewerage or even for septic tanks. The question of whether the town would pay for a sewerage system went to a plebiscite—and most ratepayers voted against it, seeing it as too expensive during the depression. Hotels in the region were nonetheless obligated by the licensing board to provide septic tank systems, with the board stating that:

> If the ratepayers of Kyneton were prepared to deny to them selves a proper sanitary service for their town, they would not be allowed to deny that right to the travelling public. ("Country Section", *The Age*, June 25, 1936)

The Kyneton discussion referred to similar decisions in other country areas. Licensing requirements for toilets and urinals for hotels through the board-dominated "swill" era created a disjunction between pre-liberalisation and post-1987 licensed venues. Earlier hotels had ample (sometimes cavernous) bathrooms, while those licensed after 1987 tended to only meet standard health and building regulations for toilet provisions in restaurants. The fact that health and building regulations have their own requirements for licensed facilities, and that the Environmental Protection Act also monitors septic tanks in country hotels, is another reminder of the multiple layers of policy that shape alcohol in place and space.

The former Old England Hotel in Barker Creek, meanwhile, is now a home, and is zoned Rural Living Zone (RLZ): a zone whose purpose is "to provide for residential use in a rural environment". Most shop and industry types are prohibited in this zone, as is housing above a very low density. Hotels are allowed, subject to permits, under conditions of siting, parking, and others that the site would be unlikely to meet. Any existing use rights for a hotel have long since lapsed. The site is also under a heritage overlay in the planning scheme, meaning it would be difficult to impossible to substantially change the hotel building.

The surroundings of Barkers Creek have changed since the 1920s: most notably the escalation of car traffic including the construction of a freeway bypass some years ago, with the Calder Freeway now occupying much of what once was the middle of Harcourt. The occupants of the area have also changed, at least in part—with newer tree changers and commuters. But it is still basically a nineteenth-century semi-rural town in a setting of bushland and old goldfields. This colonial scene itself is one which violently displaced and disguised Indigenous history and Indigenous custodians, via a system of land demarcation. Zoning and other controls combine to make the layout of the scene much the same as in the temperance era, save for the integration of cars, and unlikely to change in terms of buildings and land uses. Ultimately, combined with objection rights, a pub is about as unlikely to be built in Barkers Creek now as it was in 1876 when local option provisions first began to escalate.

References

Anderson, D. M., Crost, B., & Rees, D. I. (2016). Wet laws, drinking establishments and violent crime. *The Economic Journal, 128*(611), 1333–1366.

Atkins, P. (2016). Animal wastes and nuisances in nineteenth-century London. In *Animal cities* (pp. 33–66). London: Routledge.

Baar, K. (1992). The national movement to halt the spread of multifamily housing, 1890–1926. *Journal of the American Planning Association, 58*(1), 39–48.

Blandy, S. (2006). Gated communities in England: Historical perspectives and current developments. *GeoJournal, 66*(1), 15–26.

Booth, P. (2002). From property rights to public control: The quest for public interest in the control of urban development. *Town Planning Review, 73*(2), 153–170.

Booth, P. (2005). The nature of difference: Traditions of law and government and their effects on planning in Britain and France. In *Comparative planning cultures* (pp. 259–284). London: Routledge.

Brenner, J. F. (1974). Nuisance law and the industrial revolution. *Journal of Legal Studies, 3*(2), 403–433.

Brinkley, C., & Vitiello, D. (2013). From farm to nuisance: Animal agriculture and the rise of planning regulation. *Journal of Planning History, 13*(2), 113–135. https://doi.org/10.1177/1538513213507542.

Burke, M. I., & Schmidt, A. (2009). The death and life of great Australian music: Planning for live music venues in Australian cities. *State of Australian Cities Conference 2009.*

Burke, M., & Schmidt, A. (2013). How should we plan and regulate live music in Australian cities? Learnings from Brisbane. *Australian Planner, 50*(1), 68–78.

Cook, N., Taylor, E., Hurley, J., & Colic-Peisker, V. (2012). Resident third party objections and appeals against planning applications: Implications for higher density and social housing-positioning paper. *AHURI Positioning Paper Series, 145*, 1–45.

Deng, F. F. (2003). The rebound of private zoning: Property rights and local governance in urban land use. *Environment and Planning A, 35*(1), 133–149.

Dennis, R. (1998, March). Apartment housing in Canadian cities 1900–1940. *Urban History Review, 26*(2), 17–31.

Dennis, R. (2000). 'Zoning' before zoning: The regulation of apartment housing in early twentieth century Winnipeg and Toronto. *Planning Perspectives, 15*, 267–299.

Douglas, M. (2003). *Purity and danger: An analysis of concepts of pollution and taboo*. London: Routledge.

Dunstan, K. (1968). *Wowsers: Being an account of the prudery exhibited by certain outstanding men and women in such matters as drinking, smoking, prostitution, censorship and gambling*. Melbourne, VIC: Cassel Australia.

Fernandez, J., Gohmann, S., & Pinkston, J. C. (2018). Breaking bad in Bourbon country: Does alcohol prohibition encourage methamphetamine production? *Southern Economic Journal, 84*(4), 1001–1023.

Fischel, W. A. (2004). An economic history of zoning and a cure for its exclusionary effects. *Urban Studies, 41*(2), 340–371.

Fogelson, R. (2005). *Bourgeois nightmares: Suburbia, 1870–1930*. New Haven, CT: Yale University Press.

Forge, W. (1985). *The Wade House case*. Waterloo, NSW: McCulloch Waterloo Press.

Freestone, R., & Grubb, M. (1998). The Melbourne metropolitan town planning commission, 1922–30. *Journal of Australian Studies, 22*(57), 128–144.

Garnett, N. S. (2005, September). Relocating disorder. *Virginia Law Review, 91*(5), 1076–1112.

Hamlin, C. (1988). Muddling in bumbledom: On the enormity of large sanitary improvements in four British towns, 1855–1885. *Victorian Studies, 32*(1), 55–83.

Hirt, S. A. (2015). *Zoned in the USA: The origins and implications of American land-use regulation*. Ithaca, NY: Cornell University Press.

Homan, S. (2011). "I Tote and I Vote": Australian live music and cultural policy. *Arts Marketing: An International Journal, 1*(2), 96–107.

Hurley, J., Taylor, E., & Dodson, J. (2017). Getting dense: Why has urban consolidation been so difficult? In *The Routledge handbook of Australian urban and regional planning*. New York: Routledge.

Jacobs, H. M., & Paulsen, K. (2009). Property rights: The neglected theme of 20th-century American planning. *Journal of the American Planning Association, 75*(2), 134–143.

Johnson, R. (2005). Law and the leaky woman: The saloon, the liquor licence, and narratives of containment. *Continuum, 19*(2), 181–199.

Kiechle, M. (2016). Navigating by nose: Fresh air, stench nuisance, and the urban environment, 1840–1880. *Journal of Urban History, 42*(4), 753–771.

Lewis, M. (1991). *A rum state: Alcohol and state policy in Australia 1988–1988*. Australian Government Publication Service.
Livingston, M. (2017). *Packaged liquor in Victoria: 2001 to 2016*. Canberra: Foundation for Alcohol Research and Education.
McComas, M. (2016). "Zoning" in on Maryland's nascent marijuana industry. *University of Baltimore Journal of Land and Development, 5*(2), 5.
McKernan, M. (1983). *All in! Australia during the Second World War*. Melbourne: Nelson.
Melbourne and Metropolitan Board of Works. (1954). *Melbourne Metropolitan Planning Scheme 1954*. Accessed from: http://www.dtpli.vic.gov.au/planning/plans-and-policies/planning-for-melbourne/melbournes-strategic-planning-history/melbourne-metropolitan-planning-scheme-1954.
Melbourne and Metropolitan Board of Works. (1959). *Melbourne Metropolitan Planning Scheme Ordinance, Public Records Office Victoria Series 16157—Melbourne Metropolitan Planning Scheme Ordinance and Interim Development Orders, Reprints and Amendments.*
Merrett, D. T. (1979). The victorian licensing court 1906–68: A study of role and impact. *Australian Economic History Review, 19*(2), 123–150.
Meyer, W. B., & Brown, M. (1989). Locational conflict in a nineteenth-century city. *Political Geography Quarterly, 8*(2), 107–122.
Moore, S. A. (2012). Garbage matters: Concepts in new geographies of waste. *Progress in Human Geography, 36*(6), 780–799.
Németh, J., & Ross, E. (2014). Planning for marijuana: The cannabis conundrum. *Journal of the American Planning Association, 80*(1), 6–20.
Nieuwenhuysen, J. (1988). Liquor control policy and alcohol availability—Consumption relationships: Reflections on the Victorian debate. *Australian Drug and Alcohol Review, 7*(3), 263–271.
O'Hanlon, S. (2002). *Together apart: Boarding house, hostel and flat life in pre-war Melbourne*. Melbourne: Australian Scholarly Publishing.
Oldham, P. (2013). 'Suck more piss': How the confluence of key Melbourne-based audiences, musicians, and iconic scene spaces informed the Oz rock identity. *Perfect Beat, 14*(2), 120.
Phillips, W. (1980). 'Six o'clock swill': The introduction of early closing of hotel bars in Australia. *Historical Studies, 95*(75), 251.
Rowley, S. (2017). *The Victorian planning system: Practice, problems and prospects*. Annandale, NSW: Federation Press.
Schilling, J., & Linton, L. S. (2005). The public health roots of zoning: In search of active living's legal genealogy. *American Journal of Preventive Medicine, 28*(2), 96–104.
Shaw, K. (2005). The place of alternative culture and the politics of its protection in Berlin, Amsterdam and Melbourne. *Planning Theory & Practice, 6*(2), 149–169.

Shoup, D. C. (2005). *The high cost of free parking* (Vol. 7). Washington, DC, USA: Planners Press, American Planning Association.
Shumsky, N. L., & Springer, L. M. (1981). San Francisco's zone of prostitution, 1880–1934. *Journal of Historical Geography, 7*(1), 71–89.
Taylor, E. J. (2013). Do house values influence resistance to development?—A spatial analysis of planning objection and appeals in Melbourne. *Urban Policy and Research, 31*(1), 5–26.
Taylor, E. J. (2015). Fast food planning conflicts in Victoria 1969–2012: Is every unhappy family restaurant unhappy in its own way? *Australian Planner, 52*(2), 114–126.
Taylor, E. J., Cook, N., & Hurley, J. (2016). Do objections count? Estimating the influence of residents on housing development assessment in Melbourne. *Urban Policy and Research, 34*(3), 1–15.
Taylor, E. J., & Rowley, S. (2017). *Written in pencil or in ink: Private covenants and their legacies for housing and planning in Victoria*. Adelaide: State of Australian Cities (SOAC) 2017.
Thomas, J. M., & Ritzdorf, M. (1997). Village of Euclid v. Ambler Realty Corporation (1926). In J. M. Thomas & M. Ritzdorf, (Ed.), *Urban planning and the African American community: In the shadows*. Thousand Oaks, London, and New Delhi: Sage.
Valverde, M. (1998). *Diseases of the will: Alcohol and the dilemmas of freedom*. Cambridge and New York: Cambridge University Press.
Victorian Prohibition League. (1930). *Picture—"BOOZE: The SHADOW over our land: Vote YES and remove it [picture]"*. http://handle.slv.vic.gov.au/10381/103274.

Newspaper Articles

"Local option in England". *South Australian Register*, June 30, 1883.
"Local option poll: Postponement resented". *The Argus*, December 13, 1922.
"Country section". *The Age*, June 25, 1936, p. 9. http://nla.gov.au/nla.news-article204832074.
The Argus, April 28, 1944.
The Age, March 13, 1950.
"Move to oppose hotel at Box Hill". *The Age*, April 21, 1950.
"Dry area might get 'reprieve'". *The Argus*, December 3, 1953.
"Bark Hut and Ti-Tree Village holiday park in Ocean Grove forced to close because of old prohibition law". *Herald Sun*, October 25, 2012.
"Community rejects bottle shop by school". *Sydney Morning Herald*, August 4, 2013. http://www.smh.com.au/nsw/community-rejects-bottle-shop-by-school-20130803-2r663.html.

"Cheers to end of booze ban: VCAT rules covenant no longer enforceable". *Geelong Advertiser*, March 13, 2014.
"End to dry polls for Melbourne cafes and restaurants". *The Age*, May 13, 2015.
The Age, May 16, 2015.
"Newsagent's alcohol license angers pub free Bourneville". *The Guardian*, October 1, 2015.

Australasian Legal Information Institute (AUSTLII)—Legal Records

Victorian Historic Acts
Licensing Act 1922. http://www.austlii.edu.au/cgi-bin/viewdb//au/legis/vic/hist_act/la1922104/.
Licensing Amendment Act 1949. http://www.austlii.edu.au/cgi-bin/viewdb//au/legis/vic/hist_act/la1949184/.
Licensing Amendment Act 1953. http://www.austlii.edu.au/au/legis/vic/hist_act/la1953184/.
Licensing Act 1958. http://www.austlii.edu.au/cgi-bin/viewdb//au/legis/vic/hist_act/la1958104/.
Licensing Act 1965. http://www.austlii.edu.au/cgi-bin/viewdb//au/legis/vic/hist_act/la1965104/.
Liquor Control (Amendment) Act 1968. http://www.austlii.edu.au/cgi-bin/viewdb//au/legis/vic/hist_act/lca1968277/.
Liquor Control (Amendment) Act 1979. http://www.austlii.edu.au/cgi-bin/viewdb//au/legis/vic/hist_act/lca1979277/.
Liquor Control Act 1983. http://www.austlii.edu.au/cgi-bin/viewdb//au/legis/vic/hist_act/lca1983197/.
Liquor Control Act 1987. http://www.austlii.edu.au/cgi-bin/viewdb//au/legis/vic/hist_act/lca1987197/.
Liquor Control Reform Act 1998. http://www8.austlii.edu.au/cgi-bin/viewdb/au/legis/vic/consol_act/lcra1998266/.

Decisions
Victorian Civil and Administrative Tribunal (VCAT). (2012, October 10). *McDonald's Australia Pty Ltd v Yarra Ranges SC [2012] VCAT 1539.* http://www.austlii.edu.au/au/cases/vic/VCAT/2012/1539.html.
Victorian Civil and Administrative Tribunal (VCAT). (2013, May 20). *Hunt Club Commercial Ply Ltd v Casey CC (includes Summary) (Red Dot) [2013] VCAT 725.* http://www.austlii.edu.au/au/cases/vic/VCAT/2013/725.html.
Victorian Civil and Administrative Tribunal (VCAT). (2014, March 4). *Linaker v Greater Geelong CC [2014] VCAT 236.* http://www8.austlii.edu.au/cgi-bin/viewdoc/au/cases/vic/VCAT/2014/236.html.

Victorian Civil and Administrative Tribunal (VCAT). (2016, September 19). *Mylonas v Darebin CC [2016] VCAT 1583.* http://www.austlii.edu.au/cgi-bin/viewdoc/au/cases/vic/VCAT/2016/1583.html.
Victorian Supreme Court (VSC). (2012, January 11). *Prowse v Johnstone & Ors [2012] VSC 4.* Victorian Supreme Court. http://www.austlii.edu.au/au/cases/vic/VSC/2012/4.html.

CHAPTER 5

The Highland Society: Hair of the Dog

Abstract In this chapter Taylor argues that the often overlooked "local option" policies introduced through the temperance movement of the late nineteenth and early twentieth centuries form part of the genealogy of zoning and planning. The early twenty-first century is a useful time to reflect on this history, as while some temperance era controls are being reformed or scaled back, essentially identical controls are put forward apparently for much the same reasons. The chapter shows how contemporary planning debates around alcohol-related land uses, and other developments seen as polluting, re-enact local option debates. Examples of divisive bottle shop and electronic gaming machine developments (including the Highland Society proposal in Castlemaine) are given. The chapter critically examines ways in which tensions between individual and local rights, as between localism and centralism; the promise and perils of direct democratic rights; and the persistence of domestic violence, continue to catalyse local controls on alcohol.

Keywords Urban history · Planning history · Direct democracy · Domestic violence · Gaming machines · NIMBY

The idiomatic expression "hair of the dog" refers to the tempting belief that a hangover may be cured by further drinking. The previous chapters have identified hangovers for land use planning systems from the temperance era in Victoria. This final chapter considers how the early

© The Author(s) 2019

E. J. Taylor, *Dry Zones*, https://doi.org/10.1007/978-981-13-2787-2_5

twenty-first century is a useful time to reflect on temperance history, given that at the same time some temperance era controls are being scaled back, essentially identical controls are being put forward for what appear to be much the same reasons. Similar debates as the temperance era are being re-enacted not only around alcohol-related land uses (e.g. the *Hunt Club* big box bottle shop); but around new land uses seen as polluting or nuisances: gaming machines, wind turbines, cannabis outlets (in Canada and the United States), fast food restaurants and others.

In 2010 in Castlemaine, a few kilometres down the road from Harcourt and Barkers Creek (see Fig. 1.1), the Maryborough Highland Society sought planning permission for a licensed club with 65 electronic gaming machine ("pokies"). The proposal, in a region famously divided between older residents and recent tree changers, was immediately as divisive as local option had been in the area in the late nineteenth century. A protest group, "Enough Pokies in Castlemaine" (EPIC), was formed to contest the proposal. In a drawn-out battle waged through various stages of planning, liquor and gaming approvals, over 500 protest submissions were submitted. In their campaigns EPIC even staged singing demonstrations, a direct mirror of WCTU tactics. The Victorian Commission for Gambling Regulation noted:

> The range and intensity of community opposition, and perceptions of a change to the social character of Castlemaine through a trebling of gaming machines in the town through a single approval.
>
> Mount Alexander SC v Victorian Commission for Gambling and Liquor Regulation & Ors (includes Summary) [2013] VCAT 101. (February 14, 2013b)

Gaming Machines were illegal in Victoria until 1992. While legalised after that point, they have always been tightly regulated, and are only allowed in venues with liquor licenses. Victoria has a total cap on numbers of the machines; and an in-built duopoly system wherein two major operators own all machines and hotels and clubs bid to host them (Marshall and Baker 2001). As of 2006 Victoria also has per-capita caps on pokies by region (as per the statutory limit on hotels of the nineteenth century); and for new machines requires an assessment of benefits and disbenefits to the community. Venues with machines also require car parking (0.4 spaces for each patron permitted; or 3.5 for each 100 sqm).

A portion of gaming revenue goes to designated purposes, including a Community Support Fund (in the style of Samlag laws) but gaming revenue is also a substantial contributor to general state revenue. Thus in many respects gaming machine regulations seem to be informed, consciously or otherwise, by temperance era ideas for regulating alcohol and mitigating its costs.

Marshall and Baker (2001) found the distribution of gaming machines in Victoria partly reflects the effects of the local option polls and the dearth of hotels in some areas (p. 84)—partly because the machines have to be located in hotels or clubs, Boroondara and Nunawading have the fewest gaming machines. Gaming machines have become disproportionately located in lower socio-economic areas, through a combination of factors including the duopoly system, and the requirement for gaming machines must be hosted in licensed hotels and clubs. Early on, the machines clustered in areas with licensed venues with extensive parking, and where the gaming machine operators saw greatest profit. Regional limits were introduced only in 2006. Conflict over gaming machines has primarily been around new machines—as, for example, in the Castlemaine Highland Society proposal. In these cases the decision-making process considers social and economic benefits and disbenefits; the idea of density and there being sufficient poker machines in an area already; whether new machines are needed or not needed in an area; and the number of objections against the proposal. Again these are close matches to earlier liquor licensing controls (see Chapter 3).

In the Castlemaine case, the machines were ultimately denied permits—the Victorian Commission for Gambling and Liquor Regulation determined that they would have more costs than benefits to the Castlemaine community. And while the decision distanced itself from the idea of a referendum or plebiscite, indirectly it supported the idea of the scale of community opposition being a valid consideration around gaming, with the commission acknowledging that:

> Some of EPIC's witness evidence has been of assistance to the Tribunal, and the range and intensity of opposition to this proposal, whether rational or irrational, has been a relevant factor in assessing the net impact on the well-being of the community.
>
> VCAT (2013), Mount Alexander SC v Victorian Commission for Gambling and Liquor Regulation & Ors [2013] VCAT 101. (February 14, 2013b)

Interpretations of the *Gambling Regulation Act 2003* provide for the number of local objections to new gaming machines being sufficient grounds to refuse permission—this principle was established by a dispute over machines proposed for a hotel in another country town, Romsey, in 2008 (VSCA 2008). In the Romsey debate in 2008, the Supreme Court in Victoria upheld community opposition to a poker machine development in the town's only pub. The Court effectively determined that the amount of opposition *did* count as social impact. Recently, the last hotel in Romsey was closed, seemingly not without a touch of spite on the part of the owner who surmised that "old-fashioned hotels are finished" (meaning hotels without pokies), and suggested the site would likely become a fast food outlet ("Romsey Pub Calls It a Day", *Star Weekly*, October 17, 2017; "No Plans to Reopen 'Eyesore' Romsey Hotel", *Macedon Ranges Leader*, January 17, 2018).

In Victoria today a licensed club with gaming machines would need a planning permit; a liquor license; a gaming machine permit—and a planning permit for the liquor license (and gaming machines)—with attendant car parking provision and debates over social impacts for most of these elements. Whatever one's view on gaming or alcohol, this still amounts to an extraordinary level of regulation and applies disproportionately (though not exclusively) to the vice issues that the temperance movement railed against. (Admittedly, Castlemaine also managed to be deeply divided over a proposed supermarket.) Planning and associated regulations are intended to reduce social impacts of developments and provide forums for community input. Yet Marshall and Baker (2001) surmised that some of the spatial effects have been unintended and negative, that:

> Gaming laws designed with specific objectives in mind appear to be exacerbating the concentration of gaming machines into disadvantaged areas. (p. 89)

Recent planning debates over alcohol-related land uses—notably bottle shop densities—as well as around such diffuse land uses as fast food outlets, apartments, wind turbines and gaming machines have corollaries in the temperance era. They are both informed by, and re-enacting, temperance era debates. Some debates are over increasing land uses seen as increasingly problematic and evoking public health arguments; others (gaming machines, or cannabis outlets in some US states and Canadian provinces) have been recently legalised, leading immediately to questions of where and on what basis they are to be located. Some, as in the case of cannabis, are still prohibited in Australia despite (as with US national prohibition on alcohol) criminalising a significant portion of the adult population. Many of the new foes and fears that communities use the planning system to oppose are also products, in part, of zoning and regulation. Around these and other issues, popular pressures are increasingly demanding temperance-style restrictions and rights. The fact that despite many moves toward liberalisation, similar dilemmas and fears return, has implications for how the temperance era is understood.

5.1 Direct Local Democracy: Freedom or Its Opposite?

Significant changes to alcohol supply and consumption in Victoria have occurred since the time of the temperance movement in Victoria. But even after liberalising reforms in both liquor and planning regulation, certain localised controls on alcohol remain, while others are being reintroduced. Popular pressures for direct local democratic rights (such as plebiscites and referendums) are being reasserted, with local and central governments often in tension around this question. Elsewhere (Taylor 2015) I argued that these illustrate Massey's idea of defensive localism increasing as a corollary to globalisation. Even–perhaps especially—in a globalised world, the role of the local and boundaries retains potency. It matters more than ever where boundaries are set, who is in, and who gets to decide. Alcohol policies, like planning, are microcosms of this.

Local restrictions on alcohol as with zoning (Fischel 2004; Hirt 2015) have often arisen from a popular demand for regulation. Temperance proponents used nascent planning laws—property rights, municipal corporations power, residential zoning—to legitimise the use of local popular political power, and to apply their rights as property owners to control alcohol. Localism, Clarke (2009) emphasises, "has sources other than statecraft". Recently in NSW, affluent North Sydney councils successfully resisted forced amalgamations. Some of the wealthiest parts of Melbourne elected to be dry areas under local option. In the temperance era proponents of local option and dry areas openly associated alcohol restrictions with liberty and rights, not control (e.g. "Local Option and Liberty", *Frankston and Somerville Standard*, Friday October 28, 1938).

Key to the influence of local option ideals in the temperance era was the premise that local communities ought to be able to have direct say in what happened in their area. Local option laws were propelled by asserted rights. Yet opponents of local option were acutely aware that restrictions bought about by local consensus could threaten individual rights. They were also aware that populist local laws could conflict with the interests of capital, and of central governments. Are local rights an extension of individual and property rights, or a threat to them? There is no easy answer to this: in liberal democratic ideals, fundamental individual rights include the right to assemble and to exclude. But these rights then become infringements on individual rights. Asserted individual rights sometimes see, somewhat perversely, an increase in the role of the state.

The popular appeal of local direct democracy today comes with a cautionary tale from local option. In the temperance era, calls for local collective rights in alcohol policy deeply divided political parties—even at the same time as they formed unlikely but powerful alliances. The English equivalent of local option, the Permissive Bill, divided the Liberal Party between proponents of local democratic rights, and critics wary of the coercive impact of the majority on individual liberties (Nicholls 2006; Nicholson 1990; Dingle 1980). In the United States, local veto was valorised as ultimate democracy and criticised as ultimate despotism—a "new and anti-American kind of majority" (Volk 2009). Volk argued that in the US local option laws have tended to be remembered only as a minor part of broader prohibition politics, but in fact revealed:

> …a more complex mixture of both popular and elite participants struggling with whether majority rule and popular political empowerment always embodied democracy or freedom, or potentially their opposites. (Volk 2009, The perils of 'pure democracy': minority rights, liquor politics, and popular sovereignty in Antebellum America, 2009, p. 647)

Volk details how US temperance reformers positioned liquor as enslaving and the process of removing it as liberating; and advocated local option laws as "purely democratic" "beacons of freedom and emblems of democracy", evoking popular concepts of popular self-rule. US temperance campaigners "placed popular political empowerment at the centre of their agenda" (Volk, p. 655).

The model of alcohol controls that nineteenth-century Liberal politicians like Harcourt and Burns endorsed was local-level, democratic controls. They argued that choosing (as in a local vote) was different to having rules imposed by a central government. By contrast others, linked local option controls on alcohol to religious prosecution—to the coercive power of a protestant majority (Dingle, p. 23). British Liberal Party leader Harcourt lost his seat over the issue in 1895. John Stuart Mill argued strongly for local government, but also argued that drinking and drunkenness, when they do not violate the rights of others, have no grounding to be regulated. Liberal opponents used Mills' own argument against slavery that one could not be "free to be not free" against alcohol—pitching alcohol as a lack of freedom and something no-one could rationally choose (Nicholls 2006, p. 137). Critics of Mill argued alcohol abuse in practice *did* violate the liberties of others. Burns argued that Mill was commenting on liquor "in his closet", "because he does not understand it"—that is, the impacts on the ground.

Although the British debates were divisive and the Permissive Bill defeated on numerous occasions, a common principle that gave it momentum was the principle of local self-rule. Australian debates around local option were also concerned with a community's own interests and its rights to decide its own affairs. A recent manifestation of this is the principle of localism and, in the UK, the Localism Act. The term *localism* was not used in the temperance era, but local option debates hinged on recognisable elements of it. Proponents of local option emphasised the gradual and democratic features of local alcohol controls. Like planning, localism—borders—can be conservative and progressive, a medium for change and a barrier to it, market driven or market disrupting.

The same calls for community rights are seen in alcohol policy today and in a broader sweep of land use conflicts and in the politics of new localism (e.g. Clarke 2009). Booth (2005) traced a constant tension between local and central government introduced to the English system through the 1835 Municipal Corporations Act. In the UK under the new localism agenda, alcohol researchers have asserted the importance of local-based responses to alcohol, including the local regulation of outlet densities. Haydock (2014) argues that the localism agenda explicitly encourages this response. The 2008 UK Licensing Act transferred licensing to local authorities, in line with temperance arguments around local option in the late nineteenth century (Kneale and French 2008, p. 234). In Australia also there is increasing political pressure on local liquor licensing decisions (Livingston et al. 2007).

In the United States, west coast states have long histories of direct democracy (propositions and referenda) on urban issues (Goebel 1997), including a recent resurgence for direct local democracy ideals around transport questions and urban autonomy coming from heterogeneous motives (Boudreau 2003). While not local level, Australia in 2017 had its first contemporary and very controversial plebiscite, on same-sex marriage.

In the Tecoma McDonalds case in Victoria, locals asserted that the number of objections (over a thousand) to a proposed fast food outlet ought to prevent the restaurant being approved. They were unsuccessful in this claim—however in political response to this, and to another case involving objections to an apartment tower (VSC 2013, Stonnington City Council v Lend Lease Apartments), Victoria's *Recognising Objectors Bill* was introduced in late 2015. The bill formalised popular opinion that the simple number of local objections should count, and that they did not previously was undemocratic (Taylor et al. 2016). Although probably more symbolic than instrumental (Rowley 2017), it reflects similar ideals as local option in the temperance era. It seemed to pick up on expectations, based on gaming legislation, from cases that had weighted community objections against gaming machine applications. Under the *Recognising Objectors Bill* the number of objections must be explicitly taken into account in planning permit decisions. Balancing local opinion and majority rules against other interests remains a pressing question in Victoria and elsewhere.

5.2 Big Box-Ers: Violence and Alcohol in Place

Tribunal cases in Victoria such as *Hunt Club* demonstrate not only the complex regulation of alcohol but how concerns about violence—a catalyst for much temperance activity—have also emerged again in new narratives around alcohol. "Statutory numbers" are recognisable in Victoria's recent "cumulative impact" and "designated areas" measures, freezes and lockouts on late night venues, and in concerns about bottle shops and their links to domestic violence.

In caricatures of the nanny state, and in caricatured memory of the wowser, controls on alcohol are binaries between invasive government and morality on the one side, and individual rights on the other. Temperance proponents were often propelled by moral or medicalised beliefs, and this is how they are largely remembered. To many, temperance was a deeply conservative, religious, middle-class value system invasively asserted onto public life. The track record of the temperance movement with instigating judgemental and exclusionary controls on alcohol underscores much of the subsequent critical perspectives on it.

Thus temperance, in hindsight, is sometimes understood only as an imposition of middle-class values. Eric Hobsbawn describes "mass 'alcoholism'" as "an almost invariable companion of headlong and uncontrolled industrialisation". Class is a recurring theme in alcohol and its regulation. Yet taking a class-based view seems to often involve—for unclear reasons—editing out or minimising the role of interpersonal violence, particularly gendered violence, in giving momentum to temperance movements. The pivotal role of working-class women and—more recently—indigenous women in calls for local alcohol controls unsettles a binary of alcohol policy along only class or race lines. For example Wright (2014) observes how:

> As it was with other parts of the western world, Temperance in the Australian colonies was in many ways an expression of middle class concern about the socially disruptive effects of alcohol, most of which were perpetrated, or experienced, by the working class. But many members of the working class, and especially women (who so often suffered the brunt of economic and family deprivation resulting from alcohol abuse) strongly supported Temperance aims and activities. (Wright 2014, p. 195)

I began this book by describing one of great-great-grandfathers, Jack Wilkinson, a drinker and someone with a violent criminal record, and how his example influenced one part of my family into becoming non-drinkers active in the temperance movement. Responding to violence with critical if simplistic views on alcohol was not unique to my family, nor is it an attitude confined to the past.

There were no shortages of domestic assaults and homicides in the nineteenth century with which to fuel links between drinking and domestic violence, spurious or not. Drawing on court records Tomes (1978) and Pleck (1989) illustrate the widespread nature and acceptance of wife beating over centuries past, but also show how prevailing understandings of domestic violence shifted over time. During the temperance era there was a sudden and historically unusual interest in both acknowledging and legally punishing domestic violence. Tomes (1978) points to a changing middle-class attitude toward the acceptability and "manliness" of domestic violence through the mid-nineteenth century. Pleck (1989) attributes part of the sudden interest in domestic violence during the temperance era to social upheaval: combined temperance and anti-violence measures were marshalled, Pleck argues, around shared fears of immigrants, blacks, and hobos (itinerant men) "unable to control their aggressive and criminal impulses" (p. 36). Thus for a time temperance, law and order, and domestic violence concerns converged through moral panic. They also overlapped with tighter trespassing laws and early by-laws and zoning.

In *Larrikins*, Bellanta (2012) details moral panic over gangs of "larrikins"—a pejorative term for a street-based Australian subculture of working-class youth, predominantly male, in the late nineteenth and early twentieth centuries. The panic drew upon real incidents before the courts—including violent rapes—and were amplified (as compared to other sexual crimes—Smaal 2013) by public anxieties about immigration and social change. Bellanta is critical of twentieth-century broadly Marxist scholarship which implied that, because the larrikin events were the subject of *disproportionate* attention, larrikin violence was *itself* an invention of class prejudice.

A similar view of alcohol and domestic violence would be that it should be possible to accept that violence exists, and also acknowledge that interests in such violence have social and class catalysts. A different challenge would be to accept that attempts to regulate alcohol on the basis of concerns about social impacts do not necessarily have the intended effects. Kantor and Straus (1987) argue that drunkenness as a or the primary cause of male violence is an idea prevalent since the temperance era, and one that persists in folk narratives of the "drunken bum theory of wife beating". Today as during the temperance era, the root causes of interpersonal violence defy easy explanations—or at least solutions. In the absence of them, alcohol seems as likely as anything to be put forward, particularly when bundled with broader social anxieties.

Liquor law in Victoria has several newly integrated components based on concerns about violence. All have been explicitly framed as responding to violence. While some alcohol policies refer to public violence generally by males against males—as in "one punch" inspired lockout laws, the discussion of bottle shops ("packaged liquor outlets") policy more often refers to domestic violence. Since 2008 authorities have been required to consider "cumulative impact"—"the cumulative impact of any existing licensed premises and the proposed licensed premises on the amenity of the surrounding area". These can be positive or negative. Cumulative impact—with its emphasis on local numbers—evokes the statutory limits of the nineteenth century. McNamara and Quilter

(2015) show how while public drinking and drunkenness has always been effectively criminalised, narratives around it have shifted from the "street sweeping" of habits and people seen as degenerate, to a more recent anxiety associating public drinking with threats of violence.

Initial guidelines for cumulative impact guidelines in Victoria's planning provisions did suggest that cumulative impact included "violence and perceived threats to safety" as well as "anti-social behaviour from intoxicated persons". However, in a high profile case (VCAT 2013a—*Hunt Club Commercial Pty Ltd v Casey CC [2013] VCAT 725*), Victoria's planning tribunal considered the legal question of whether "social harm caused by alcohol, the accessibility of alcohol in the community generally, or the potential for the abuse or misuse of alcohol" was a valid planning consideration. The finding was that it would "rarely (if ever)" be relevant when assessing permit applications for licensed premises. Further the tribunal asserted that "town planning is not a panacea for all perceived social ills" and "town planning does not involve itself in moral judgements". This is a clear yet historically extraordinary comment given that the term "morals" was integral to the *Euclid v Ambler* decision validating zoning powers and thus planning to protect "public health, safety, morals, and general welfare" (quoted in Thomas and Ritzdorf 1997, p. 281). Perhaps it ought not to be the case that planning involves itself in morals, but in practice it long has—all but intrinsically. Liquor laws, especially, are hybrids of rationales.

In Melbourne and other suburban areas there are calls from local councils, communities, police, and medical researchers to limit the density of licensed venues and particularly bottle shops, based largely on concerns about violence. Australia also had a 2016 Senate Inquiry on the topic of "The Need for a Nationally-Consistent Approach to Alcohol-Fuelled Violence". The Victorian Royal Commission into Family Violence tabled its findings in March 2016. One of its 227 specific recommendations was to recognise domestic violence impacts in liquor licensing and planning decisions: to review legislation in order to "consider family violence and alcohol-related harms" and that this consideration "should involve consultation with people who have expertise in the inter-relationship between family violence and alcohol use" (State of Victoria 2016).

At the local level, other examples of policies seeking to tackle violence through alcohol include the Melbourne municipality of Maroondah passing a local "liquor accord", "cracking down on alcohol-fuelled violence and anti-social behaviour, in a bid to make local streets safer" (Maroondah Leader, November 29, 2015). And further afield, the Indian state of Bahir introduced statewide prohibition from 2016 "in response to a spike in violence against women", particularly rape and the rape of children ("Indian State Bans Alcohol to Curb Violence", *The New Daily*, November 25, 2015).

Concerns about violence—a catalyst for much temperance activity—have been strongly voiced around bottle shops (takeaway alcohol sales) in recent years. There is evidence that packaged liquor, and particularly chain liquor is associated with harm and disproportionately in disadvantaged areas (Livingston 2011; Morrison et al. 2016). Livingston (2011) matched outlet density to domestic violence, finding that of three major types (hotel, on-premises, packaged) only packaged alcohol density (in Melbourne, 1996–2005) had a strong positive correlation with domestic violence. A US study noted concern (but also curiosity) about "what the heck happens around US liquor stores"—pointing social interactions as a possible factor (Graham 2006). The rise of large, corporate-owned big box bottle shops has also seeded renewed debates in some Australian states: planning disputes over the social impacts of large suburban liquor stores, and controversial lockout laws limiting operating hours.

In addition, "Designated areas" were introduced to Victorian licensing legislation in 2007. These are declared by the Victorian Commission for Gambling and Liquor Regulation (VCGLR), and Chief Commissioner of Police, on the basis of crime statistics. License applications in designated areas, with around 20 declared, are subject to additional controls. The state government amended the *Victorian Commission for Gambling and Liquor Regulation Act 2011* to introduce freeze on late night (after 1 a.m.) licenses in the inner municipalities of Melbourne, Stonington, Yarra and Port Phillip. The freeze is in place until mid-2019, although some exemptions have been made available for smaller venues and those offering live music. Both the "designated areas" and inner city license freezes were prompted, as with the (more publicly controversial) lockout laws in New South Wales, by violent incidents. New South Wales' 2014 precinct-based lockout zones were introduced during a period of Federal Government interest in "alcohol-fuelled violence" following high profile deaths of young men in nightclub districts. Freezing licenses in "trouble" areas has throwbacks to the Victorian goldfields of the 1850s. Alliances between local governments and police have created "patchworks" of alcohol-free public areas, in addition to zoning restrictions on private land.

In 1991, Lewis placed temperance era connections between alcohol and violence in Australia in the past: attributing changing policy views to how "temperance analysis of, and solutions to, social problems like poverty, drunkenness and family violence now seemed misguided, or at least antiquated" (p. 69). This distancing seems to have been premature. In Australia, new alcohol policies based on—or at least seemingly prompted by—violence are again recognisable and ascendant.

Debates around violence and alcohol are not lacking in violence or domestic violence; nor in some correlations between alcohol and violence. "Alcohol-related assault" remains (as at 2005) a major police concern in Australia, with 70,000 victims annually of which 24,000 are victims of domestic violence. The public health literature points to an empirical link between the density of alcohol outlets, the lengthening of opening hours, and measures of social harm including violence (Livingston et al. 2007; Livingston 2008a, b). Kypri et al. (2011) find mitigating effects on violence from changed hours in Newcastle. Livingston (2011) finds statistical relationships between violence and outlet density particularly packaged liquor. Livingston shows clear links between density and assault in Melbourne (2008a), including changes in density over time (2008b), and also finds strong relationships between outlet density and rates of domestic violence ("family incidents" in police data) (2011). While not interrogating any claimed causality between alcohol and violence, there is clearly a role of violence in the recurrent nature of policy pressures. It may be through the endemic nature of (particularly domestic) violence that ideas about alcohol can continue to find supporters and policy at the local scale, in the nineteenth century as now.

5.3 Liberalism: "The Trouble Is the Manner of Enforcement"

In Sinclair Lewis' 1923 novel *Babbitt*, the guilelessly privileged protagonist and his friends quaff cocktails and chaff against prohibition, and ruminate on the nature of rights and liberties in matters of liquor control:

> "The trouble is the manner of enforcement," insisted Howard Littlefield. "Congress didn't understand the right system. Now, if I'd been running the thing, I'd have arranged it so that the drinker himself was licensed, and then we could have taken care of the shiftless workman – kept him from drinking – and yet not've interfered with the rights – with the personal liberty – of fellows like ourselves." They bobbed their heads, looked admiringly at one another, and stated, "That's so, that would be the stunt". (Sinclair Lewis, *Babbitt*, 1922)

Their rights, or rather "the personal liberty—of fellows like ourselves", they agree, ought not to have been subject to alcohol restrictions. Would it not have been easier instead to have limited the rights of working-class men, those less deserving of rights and liberties? "The trouble", Babbitt and friends agree as they admire each other's logic, "is the manner of enforcement".

"The manner of enforcement" seems in fact very often to be the trouble where alcohol is concerned. Likewise, with urban planning. The easy language of rights and liberty was threaded throughout early local option debates the same way it is through planning debates today. Rights are inalienable, after all, but they are also largely theoretical. In their practical details different types of rights contradict each other, and form urban politics.

The reforms of Victoria's liquor licensing system from 1987 removed the petition system, replaced by a strongly performance-based focus on "community interest" and on protecting amenity. Planning, too, was the subject of liberalisation—notably, relaxing zoning restrictions on higher density housing (Taylor 2013; Lewis 1999). Both liquor licensing and planning have been subjects of liberal reform in recent decides: but while seeking to balance residential amenity with change, neither (neo) liberalisation project has been without pushback: the tensions between local and central, individual and collective, place and property, continue to characterise planning issues including around alcohol. Unwittingly or not, similar debates and tensions as in the temperance era rise to the surface again.

Victoria's liquor licensing system has been liberalised in the sense that smaller bars, particularly in established commercial areas, are much more easily licensed now than in the twentieth century. At the same time this book has suggested that the valorisation of low-density family housing that characterised early temperance and zoning movements remains a central concern of planning systems. Pubs and other licensed venues are zoned out of residential areas; and additional protections on amenity are in place for residential areas. The same—and more—is true of the United States. Hirt (2015) surveyed the "stunning level of regulatory detail" of typical American zoning: which exclude basically everything but the single family detached home (with notable exceptions including churches and schools); regulate co-habitation of unrelated people, set minimum lot sizes and requisite amounts of car parking, and apply intricate exclusions. Hirt noted the irony of reconciling the intricately coded specifics of zoning in America; with Americans' reputation as freedom-loving individualists, asking "how such heavy government regulations [could] be acceptable in the land of political individualism" (p. 8). Broadly similar sentiments to US zoning—and to *Babbit*—are seen around Melbourne's dry zones. One resident and business owner complained that:

> I actually like living in a dry zone, we don't have any pubs or nightclubs near us, which is great, but I had to jump through so many hoops just to sell alcohol with a meal. ("Booze bans prove a real fizzer for some of Melbourne's eastern suburbs", *Herald Sun*, July 20, 2014)

"Dry zones" do seem out of place, even anachronistic, in the twenty-first-century Melbourne that is now often promoted for its proliferation of small bars and music venues. But while some legacies of the temperance era are being scaled back, new debates and policies are revisiting much the same ideas and issues. In relation to Melbourne's two dry zones, an article (*The Age*, May 16, 2015) observed that even though "laughing at wowsers" remains a popular pastime, policy issues around alcohol are still relevant and challenging a century later.

The history of local option shows that many foundation Liberal thinkers were proponents of liquor controls. Also, that the relationship between liberalism and alcohol—and local place—is far from simple. Alcohol undermines the idealised version of human nature that liberalism relies upon (Nicholson 1990). As long as there have been calls to restrict alcohol, there have been concerns about the impacts on personal liberties—and vice versa. People generally want their own liberties, but to be protected from the liberties of others. All institutionalised rights compete with other rights, and these competing rights have substantial political and practical implications. Their deployment shapes "not only the nature of political conflict, but also the kinds of publics and even the kinds of cities that are created" (Staeheli and Mitchell 2008, p. 106 quoted in Attoh 2011, p. 673). In a sense, there is little wonder that similar debates as to the temperance era reappear: they are so fundamental to colonialism, property ownership and to democracy built around it.

Both liquor licensing and planning regulations were the subjects of significant liberalisation efforts in Victoria. These reforms followed a fundamentally liberal framework of transparency and lower entry costs. The moves were also been characterised as *neo*liberal and as normalising drinking via consumer values. Broadly, the relationship between neoliberalism and alcohol is understood as devolving responsibility to individuals while maintaining markets for alcohol trade (Haydock 2014). Neoliberalism promotes individual responsible for failure even if power is not devolved (Dumas 2016).

In the abstract ideal, safeguarding the individual from the state is sufficient to balance competing interests. In this version of reality, "dilemmas" about questions like alcohol are easy to "solve". In the case of public drinking, liberalism allows people to "have fun but not to the detriment of other people's night out" (McNamara and Quilter 2015, p. 29). Abstract ideals of rationality idealise the potential for (neo)liberal approaches to easily separate and protect individual interests, including where property rights and alcohol (and especially, interpersonal violence) are concerned. The historical experience of the splintering of the Liberal party around local option—as with trends toward re-regulation and localism now—shows that liberal democratic ideals can struggle to maintain an unambiguous position on alcohol and its local regulation and rights. Fahey (1971) surmises that local option "strengthened the Liberty Party, strained it, and sometimes threatened to shatter it". The idea equally divided socialists, some of who saw a middle-class intervention in working-class lives, and others of whom saw opportunities to take local collective control of an exploitative industry (Snowden 1908, pp. 27–28).

The issues underpinning local alcohol policies, in the temperance era as now, have not been confined to questions of centralised state intervention in individual drinking patterns or their health consequences. They are Valverde's hybrids: also encompassing questions of local amenity and property rights; direct democracy; local law; majority versus individual rights; and the root causes of interpersonal violence. To Nicholls (2006), the awkward relationship between conservative social values and laissez faire deregulation is bound up with alcohol, in that:

> Alcohol has always played a critical role in this because it provided a very visible measure of the social impacts of deregulation…[it] has historically brought fissures and contradictions within liberal thought to the surface … many of the complexities and divisions within liberalism can be illustrated through an analysis of liberal debates on alcohol. (Nicholls 2006, p. 144)

Alcohol is particularly troubling ideals of rational secular debate given that intoxication sits unsettling somewhere between the cultural and natural worlds (as in Sulkunen 2002); and is connected to violence and disorder (Jayne et al. 2011) as much as it is to social cohesion. Most liberal paradigms allow for concern about violence, as it infringes on the rights of others. Consumption and intoxication itself, however, does not infringe on others. Wider discourses on alcohol often stagnate because they rarely distinguish between these rationales. Nicholls (2006) argues that broadly held concerns about drunken violence "continue to be conflated with" concerns about consumption and intoxication itself. Narratives shift, but the basic thread of regulatory impulse remains or re-emerges.

A superficial legacy from the temperance era is the term *Wowser*, an Australian pejorative for puritanical crusading that continues to be used in alcohol policy debates into the twenty-first century. Whether curiously or predictably, the collective memory of temperance seems to continue to be framed in binary terms: wowsers versus "common sense" enjoyment; prohibition versus no prohibition. Suspected signs of impinging wowserism are reflexively disavowed. In, for example, a 2015 Australian opinion piece titled "I'm no prohibitionist, but still sobriety is my most radical pleasure" (*The Guardian*, May 26, 2015), prohibition was summarised simply as "the legalised disaster we know as Prohibition". The author went on to espouse many of the same values as early temperance proponents, possibly unaware that the movement had ever proposed anything other than national prohibition. In an opinion piece critical of the effects of Sydney lockout laws (forced closures of venues at 1am in night life areas associated with violence), Barrie (2016) evoked temperance imagery by attributing the liquor licensing rules through which "everything is now illegal, including fun" to "special little people…giggling away as they pull their little regulatory levers".

An earlier opinion piece critical of changes to liquor licensing laws in Sydney (Farrelly 2014), likewise evoked liquor control as wowserism.

In "The long reaction against the wowser" Room (2010) contended that the temperance movement was more nuanced than popular memory allows, something Room attributes to deliberate obfuscation and the cultural power of the caricatured wowser. Blocker (2006) argued that the temperance movement enacted many decades of policy change, but that popular memory focuses on the failures of national prohibition. Kneale and French (2008) likewise point to recent research showing the complexity of temperance era policy and debates—noting that however "neither 'expert' nor 'lay' discussions of the current dilemma about drink seem to have learned from this research" (p. 246). They argue that simplified memories of temperance era policies mean the "contradictions and contestations are lost" (p. 246), and that this loss hampers contemporary understanding of policies and their meanings.

Similar complexities are seen in the continued popularity of zoning controls in the USA (Hirt 2015; Fischel 2004). Following historicised legal studies (as in Valverde 1998), this book has assumed that the history of rights around local alcohol controls have had influence, and say something of the forces that created them. The hangovers of the dry zones and their creators are not so easily relegated to history books: as we live in a system of urban separation and regulation devised, at least part, by them. This influence is also not so easily confined to state controls and top-down regulatory levers.

The inclination to over-simplify temperance era policy debates may be, as in Latour (2012), interpreted as reflecting a desire to mentally separate (or in his terminology, "purify") modern planning and legal systems from their pasts. Initial local alcohol laws can be interpreted as boundary making, expelling pollution from residential areas—later, these early laws seem themselves to have received the same treatment. Temperance and early town planning ideas combined religion and morality, with public health, eugenics, property rights, liberal democracy and real estate in a way that seem uncomfortable to planning and policy discourse today. To caricature temperance concerns about alcohol as pre-modern and superstitious could be a means to elevate current systems of control to the status of rational. Temperance is also popularly remembered as a specifically religious influence—whereas in a time where essentially everyone was religious (see Chapter 3), it was more accurately the influence of a particular Christian religious belief over others.

Local liquor control—like planning regulation—is not the product of a homogenous state but of a more complex set of rights and restrictions, often demanded by competing groups.

Adam Smith in *The Wealth of Nations* warned "people of the same trade seldom meet together, even for merriment and diversion, but the conversation ends in a conspiracy against the public, or in some contrivance to raise prices". The quote refers not to an argument for regulating trade but, assuming people act primarily in their own interests, to the inevitability that government regulations will be captured by those with an existing interest in them. This is prescient when applying the concept of liberalism to liquor licensing—in a space already so regulated, indeed defined by regulation.

Merrett (1979) looking at the legal history of early twentieth-century licensing law in Victoria characterised the inadvertent outcomes of higher "standards" for new hotels as creating monopoly rents. In Brisbane, designation of "entertainment precincts" has favoured and gave further monopoly power to larger landowners in the defined precincts (Burke and Schmidt 2013), increasing entry costs and forcing new venues to operate illegally. Having dipped into the strange world of regulations on alcohol, I find it is near impossible to believe that even one person has any idea what these multitude policies combine to do, how, why, and what their effects are. Once, at a presentation, an audience member, a professional auditor of government policy, told me of an obscure subsection of Queensland prostitution law—requiring that access to a brothel must allow "vehicles to enter and exit the brothel premises in forward gear" (that is, not in reverse gear) (Queensland Prostitution Regulation 2014—https://www.legislation.qld.gov.au/view/pdf/inforce/current/sl-2014-0192). Despite his best efforts even at the highest levels of government, he concluded that no-one had any idea where this rule came from or what it achieved. The no-reverse rule, like many others, survived simply because *sounded* like it would keep *something* under control, after all. Like special licensing hours for ANZAC day, these laws do seem better understood as inherited narratives.

This book has illustrated how local demand for alcohol control has been a feature of middle-class urban colonial neighbourhoods. It is also a feature of many Indigenous communities in Australia. I will conclude by looking at these briefly. The politics of alcohol controls in remote

Indigenous communities further unsettles the idea of a “left” or “right” position around local rights or alcohol.

Alcohol restrictions have long been both enforced onto, and enforced by, Indigenous communities in Australia as in other colonial countries. Prohibitions specific to Indigenous people were introduced for example in New South Wales in 1838, Victoria in 1838, South Australian in 1930, and the Northern Territory in 1933. Ostensibly a protective measure, racially defined prohibitions were a potent signifier of conscribed rights and autonomy. Complex systems distinguished those Indigenous people allowed to drink from those disallowed via the “permit to drink” in South Australia, “stud book” in the Northern Territory, and “dog tag” in Western Australia. This ascribed “right to drink openly” was “equated with citizenship” (Lewis 1991, p. 160).

The more famous (or infamous) “dry zones” are controls on public drinking: recently resurged in NSW and in patchwork usage elsewhere in Australia. Public drinking laws have long been unequally used against indigenous people (McNamara and Quilter 2015). For example the Northern Territory’s 2-kilometre law compounds discrimination in licensed venues (Healy et al. 1985). Some jurisdictions have even recently taken up Babbitt’s suggestion, registering drinkers directly. Restricting access to alcohol had a paternal basis, grounded in the assumption that Indigenous people were doomed by alcohol and needed to be protected from it. Langton (1993) explored the long-term impact of the constructed image of the “degenerate native” and “drunken Aborigine”. Langton argues such narratives, combined with drinking laws, allowed the realities of colonisation to be ignored. While relatively newly focused on violence, public drinking laws have always enforced ideas of spatial management to which Indigenous people have been especially vulnerable. To Valverde (1998), regarding similar laws in North America (Manitoba), such distinctions and narratives:

> …reminds us that a genealogy of freedom needs to include the experiences of those who have not been deemed worthy to use their own wills to govern their desires and their acts. (Valverde 1998, pp. 144–145)

Processes of industrialisation and suburbanisation were, in Australia as in North America, intrinsically linked to land tenure systems of colonialism. Land tenure is often what afforded early rights in determining local policies on alcohol. Colonialism excluded Indigenous rights, not only to land and collective identity, but at the level of alcohol access and consumption.

The role of local place-based controls in this history is complex. Prohibitions on aboriginal drinking were abolished in Australian States and Territories over the 1960s and 1970s. However, locally defined alcohol controls continued. In the Northern Territory all Aboriginal reserves were dry until 1981. Under the Liquor Act 1979 Aboriginal communities have had the option of being declared by the Liquor Commission as restricted areas. These restrictions applied to places, not people, and were voluntary—and were thus similar to temperance era local option. The provisions empowered Indigenous communities to reject alcohol, or to implement a controlled canteen system (similar to municipalisation, Gothenburg or Samlag versions of local option). As at 1983, 56 communities had taken up the restriction option (Lewis 1991). As at 2007, of the Northern Territory's hundred-plus remote indigenous communities, 80% were dry by community option under the 1979 Liquor Act and 7 ran licensed canteens.

Although the restrictions were often evaded, they nonetheless represented local decision-making on alcohol. The politics of dry Indigenous communities shifted dramatically in 2007 when the Commonwealth Government rolled out its Northern Territory Emergency Response—the "Intervention". Among other processes, the Intervention saw compulsory bans on alcohol in remote Indigenous communities. As in the temperance era, gendered violence was a catalyst for the Intervention. The 2008 report *Little Children are Sacred*, prepared by a former Children's Court Magistrate and a Crown Prosecutor, detailed cases of abuse, rape and assaults against Indigenous women and children and was used to inform the process. As in temperance era politics and in liquor policy debates more broadly, the veracity of these experiences of violence were disputed around the Intervention. Langton (2008) argued that in some respects the intervention implemented "what many have been recommending for decades: protective interventions to prevent the abuse, rape and assault of Aboriginal women and children, and decisive action against the perpetrators". Langton's interpretation of the Intervention is far from universal, with others pointing to the paternalistic and discriminatory nature of the Intervention including its bans on alcohol.

Class or minority rights are at times hostile to discussion of domestic violence or child abuse as doing so implicitly undermines the credibility of a whole group and carries the possibility of being used to justify repression. In the temperance era, there was likewise a disconnection between the street-based and narrative-based arguments of the Salvation Army, and the theories of Liberal idealists and some sides of left wing politics. Each was accused of a disconnection: the latter from the realities and gender asymmetries of violence and deprivation; the former from the unintended and perverse costs of intervening in the lives of others.

From a localism, place-based perspective, a fundamental change of the Northern Territory Intervention was that whereas 80% of the communities were already voluntarily dry, under the Intervention all were newly subject to externally imposed bans on alcohol. Local rights are significant in pushback against the Intervention, but also in advocating alcohol controls (Senate 2012). In 2012, amidst plans to roll back alcohol restrictions, a discussion piece (D'Abbs 2012) stressed the strong demand from some Aboriginal communities for self-rule on alcohol: noting that "although the unilateral and blanket geographical coverage of these restrictions angered many Aboriginal (and other) people, the principle of banning alcohol was not new". A slightly disingenuous comment underneath, alluding to the class and racial aggression of the Intervention "restricting people's freedom", asked sardonically, "would Toorak residents put up with prohibition?" The commenter was, apparently, unaware of the long history of community-voted prohibition in, if not Toorak, its immediate neighbour of Camberwell.

Re-emerging controls on the location and density of liquor outlets, based on concerns about domestic violence, have both roots and equivalents in the temperance era. Part of the impetus for such policy debates is the tradition of under-criminalising private violence and over-criminalising public disorder. Looking at such policy questions surrounding alcohol in aspatial ways misrepresents their basic workings and histories. Taking an assumption that planning practice "cannot possibly be divorced—as a rational, technical exercise—from the general traditions that inform it" (Booth 2005), in this book I have argued that liquor licensing and the temperance movement are under-acknowledged parts of the genealogy of planning practice in Australia.

In the long run the comprehensive vision of the "alcohol shall fail!" motto of the Victorian Local Option Alliance failed. But the particular brand of drinking culture that they targeted is now long gone. They may not have possessed an exact vision of the future, but the hangovers of the dry zones and their creators, the so-called wowsers, are not so easily relegated to history books. We live in a system of competing asserted rights, and of urban separation and of zoning regulations devised, at least part, by them. Cities like Melbourne were fundamentally shaped by temperance advocates, and yet would be unrecognisable to them. Melbourne today is a world of far fewer pubs, a different array of rights and highly particular regulations, more day-to-day alcohol consumption, more water fountains, and a more mind-boggling proliferation of coffee outlets than even a movement that promoted coffee palaces as alternatives to alcohol could have conceived of. Given that temperance proponents frowned on smoking only slightly less than they did drunkenness, the ascendancy of Melbourne's twenty-first-century coffee culture alongside a proliferation of small and decidedly non-smoking bars brings its own ironies. Things did not seem exactly to go to plan, but they did change: like most drinking sessions when viewed from a hangover of the following day.

References

Attoh, K. A. (2011). What kind of right is the right to the city? *Progress in Human Geography, 35*(5), 669–685.

Barrie, M. (2016). Would the last person in Sydney please turn the lights out? https://www.linkedin.com/pulse/would-last-person-sydney-please-turn-lights-out-matt-barrie. Accessed 11 April 2016.

Bellanta, M. (2012). *Larrikins: A history.* Brisbane: University of Queensland Press.

Blocker J. S. (2006). Did prohibition really work? Alcohol prohibition as a public health innovation. *American Journal of Public Health, 96*(2), 233–243.

Booth, P. (2005). The nature of difference: Traditions of law and government and their effects on planning in Britain and France. In *Comparative planning cultures* (pp. 259–284). London: Routledge.

Boudreau, J. A. (2003). Questioning the use of 'local democracy' as a discursive strategy for political mobilization in Los Angeles, Montreal and Toronto. *International Journal of Urban and Regional Research, 27*(4), 793–810.

Burke, M., & Schmidt., A. (2013). How should we plan and regulate live music in Australian cities? Learnings from Brisbane. *Australian Planner, 50*(1), 68–78.

Clarke, N. (2009). In what sense 'spaces of neoliberalism'? The new localism, the new politics of scale, and town twinning. *Political Geography, 28*(2009), 496–507.

D'Abbs. (2012). New singers, old songs: Alcohol bans in Aboriginal communities. The Conversation. https://theconversation.com/new-singers-old-songs-alcohol-bans-in-aboriginal-communities-10051.

Dingle, A. E., (1980). *The campaign for prohibition in Victorian England: The United Kingdom Alliance, 1872–1895.* Abingdon: Taylor & Francis.

Dumas, M. J. (2016). My Brother as "Problem": Neoliberal Governmentality and Interventions for Black Young Men and Boys. *Educational Policy, 30*(1), 94–113.
Fahey, D. M. (1971). Temperance and the Liberal Party—Lord Peel's Report, 1899. *The Journal of British Studies, 10*(02), 132–159.
Farrelly, E. (2014). Lock out laws shut down Sydney's Oxford Street, Sydney Morning Herald, 28 August 2014.
Fischel, W. A. (2004). An economic history of zoning and a cure for its exclusionary effects. *Urban Studies, 41*(2), 317–340.
Goebel, T. (1997). "A case of democratic contagion": Direct democracy in the American West, 1890–1920. *Pacific Historical Review, 66*(2), 213–230.
Graham, K. (2006). Isn't it time we found out more about what the heck happens around American liquor stores? *Addiction, 101*(5), 619–620.
Haydock, W. (2014). The rise and fall of the 'nudge' of minimum unit pricing: The continuity of neoliberalism in alcohol policy in England. *Critical Social Policy, 34*(2), 260–279.
Healy, B., Turpin, T., & Hamilton, M. (1985). Aboriginal drinking: a case study in inequality and disadvantage. *The Australian Journal of Social Issues, 20*(3), 191.
Hirt, S. A. (2015). *Zoned in the USA: The origins and implications of American land-use regulation*. Ithaca: Cornell University Press.
Jayne, M., Valentine, G., & Holloway, S. L. (2011). *Alcohol, drinking, drunkeness:(Dis) orderly spaces*. Aldershot: Ashgate Publishing.
Kantor, G. K., & Straus, M. A. (1987). The "drunken bum" theory of wife beating. *Social Problems, 34*(3), 213–230.
Kneale, J., & French, S. (2008, June). Mapping alcohol: Health, policy and the geographices of problem drinking in Britain. *Drugs: Education, Prevention and Policy, 15*(3), 233–249.
Kypri, K., Jones, C., Mcelduff, P., & Barker, D. (2011). Effects of restricting pub closing times on night-time assaults in an Australian city. *Addiction, 106*(2), 303–310.
Langton, M. (1993, March). Rum, seduction and death: 'Aboriginality' and alcohol. *Oceania, 63*(3), 195–206.
Langton, M. (2008). Trapped in the Aboriginal reality show. *Griffith Review, 19*, Autumn 2008, 143–162.
Latour, B. (2012). *We have never been modern*. Harvard University Press.
Lewis, S. (1922). *Babbitt*. New York: Harcourt, Brace.
Lewis, M. (1991). *A rum state: Alcohol and state policy in Australia 1988–1988*. Canberra: Australian Government Publication Service.
Lewis, M. B. (1999). *Suburban backlash: The battle for the world's most liveable city*. Hawthorn: Bloomings Books.

Livingston, M. (2008a). Alcohol outlet density and assault: A spatial analysis. *Addiction, 103*(4), 619–628.
Livingston, M. (2008b). A longitudinal analysis of alcohol outlet density and assault. *Alcoholism: Clinical and Experimental Research, 32*(6), 1074–1079.
Livingston, M. (2011). Alcohol outlet density and harm: Comparing the impacts on violence and chronic harms. *Drug and Alcohol Review, 30*(5), 515–523.
Livingston, M., Chikritzhs, T., & Room, R. (2007). Changing the density of alcohol outlets to reduce alcohol-related problems. *Drug and Alcohol Review, 26*(5), 557–566.
Marshall, D., & Baker, R. (2001). Unfair odds? Factors influencing the distribution of electronic gaming machines in Melbourne. *Urban Policy and Research, 19*(1), 77–92.
McNamara, L., & Quilter, J. (2015). Public intoxication in NSW: The contours of criminalisation. *Sydney Law Review, 37,* 1.
Merrett, D. T. (1979). The victorian licensing court 1906–68: A study of role and impact. *Australian Economic History Review, 19*(2), 123–150.
Morrison, C., Smith, K., Gruenewald, P. J., Ponicki, W. R., Lee, J. P. & Cameron, P. (2016). Relating off-premises alcohol outlet density to intentional and unintentional injuries. *Addiction, 111,* 56–64.
Nicholls, J. Q. (2006). Liberties and licenses: Alcohol in liberal thought. *International Journal of Cultural Studies, 9*(2), 131–151.
Nicholson, P. P. (1990). *The political philosophy of the British idealists: Selected studies.* Cambridge: Cambridge University Press.
Pleck, E. (1989). Criminal approaches to family violence, 1640–1980. *Crime and Justice, 11,* 19–57.
Room, R. (2010). The long reaction against the wowser: The prehistory of alcohol deregulation in Australia. *Health Sociology Review, 19*(2), 151–163.
Rowley, S. (2017). *The Victorian planning system: Practice problems and prospects.* Sydney: Federation Press.
Senate. (2012). The Senate Community Affairs Legislation Committee—Stronger Futures in the Northern Territory Bill 2011, March 2012, Commonwealth of Australia, ISBN 978-1-74229-605-0.
Smaal, Y. (2013). Historical perspectives on child sexual abuse, part 1. *History Compass, 11*(9), 702–714.
Snowden, P. (1908). *Socialism and the drink question, The Socialist Library* (Vol. 6). London: Independent Labour Party.
Sulkunen, P. (2002). Between culture and nature: Intoxication in cultural studies of alcohol and drug use. *Contemporary Drug Problems 29*(2), 253–276.
Taylor, E. J. (2013). Do house values influence resistance to development?—A spatial analysis of planning objection and appeals in Melbourne. *Urban Policy and Research, 31*(1), 5–26.

Taylor, E. J. (2015). Fast food planning conflicts in Victoria 1969–2012: Is every unhappy family restaurant unhappy in its own way? *Australian Planner, 52*(2), 114–126.

Taylor, E. J., Cook, N., & Hurley, J. (2016). Do objections count? Estimating the influence of residents on housing development assessment in Melbourne. *Urban Policy and Research, 34*(3), 1–15.

Thomas, J. M., & Ritzdorf, M. (1997). Village of euclid v. Ambler realty corporation (1926). In J. M. Thomas & M. Ritzdorf (Ed.), *Urban planning and the African American community: In the shadows*. Thousand Oaks, London, and New Delhi: Sage.

Tomes, N. (1978). A "torrent of abuse": Crimes of violence between working-class men and women in London, 1840–1875. *Journal of Social History, 11*(3), 328–345.

Valverde, M. (1998). *Diseases of the will: Alcohol and the dilemmas of freedom*. Cambridge and New York: Cambridge University Press.

Volk, K. G. (2009). The perils of 'pure democracy': Minority rights, liquor politics, and popular sovereignty in Antebellum America. *Journal of the Early Republic, 29*(4) (Winter), 641–679.

Wright, C. (2014). *Beyond the ladies lounge: Australia's female publicans*. Melbourne: Melbourne University Press.

Newspaper Articles

"Local option and liberty". *Frankston and Somerville standard*, Friday October 28, 1938.

"Romsey pub calls it a day". *Star Weekly Sunbury & Macedon Ranges*, October 17, 2017. http://www.starweekly.com.au/news/romsey-pub-calls-it-a-day/.

"No plans to reopen 'eyesore' Romsey Hotel". *Macedon Ranges Leader*, January 17, 2018.

Australasian Legal Information Institute (AUSTLII)—Legal Records

Liquor Control Act. (1987). http://www.austlii.edu.au/cgi-bin/viewdb//au/legis/vic/hist_act/lca1987197/.

Liquor Control Reform Act. (1998). http://www8.austlii.edu.au/cgi-bin/viewdb/au/legis/vic/consol_act/lcra1998266/.

Victorian Supreme Court of Appeal (VSCA). (2008). Macedon Ranges Shire Council v Romsey Hotel Pty Ltd [2008] VSCA 45. http://www.austlii.edu.au/cgi-bin/sinodisp/au/cases/vic/VSCA/2008/58.

Victorian Civil and Administrative Tribunal (VCAT). (2012). McDonald's Australia Pty Ltd v Yarra Ranges SC [2012] VCAT 1539 (10 October 2012). http://www.austlii.edu.au/au/cases/vic/VCAT/2012/1539.html.

Victorian Civil and Administrative Tribunal (VCAT). (2013a). Hunt Club Commercial Ply Ltd v Casey CC (includes Summary) (Red Dot) [2013] VCAT 725 (20 May 2013). http://www.austlii.edu.au/au/cases/vic/VCAT/2013/725.html.

Victorian Civil and Administrative Tribunal (VCAT). (2013b). Mount Alexander SC v Victorian Commission for Gambling and Liquor Regulation & Ors (includes Summary) (Red Dot) [2013] VCAT 101 (14 February 2013). http://www.austlii.edu.au/au/cases/vic/VCAT/2013/101.html.

Victorian Supreme Court (VSC). (2013). Stonnington City Council v Lend Lease Apartments (Armadale) Pty Ltd [2013] VSC 505 (19 September 2013). http://www.austlii.edu.au/au/cases/vic/VSC/2013/505.html.

CHAPTER 6

Epilogue: "HAPPY NYE, 1984"

Abstract In this chapter, Taylor concludes the study of temperance era local alcohol controls and their legacies for planning and cities today, with an epilogue revisiting the Harcourt and Barkers Creek district of central Victoria. This time the district is found many decades after the incident described in Chapter 1, and not long after the last pub has closed—partly through local option policies. Using the character of John Wilkinson, and the presence of a heritage-protected bridge, Taylor briefly reflects on the ways in which past people, ideas and politics are remembered across generations. The social influence on places by groups like the Rechabites and Methodist Church is noted, as are experiences of alcohol and of violence. Taylor asks to what extent history in liquor licensing and urban planning is forgotten, buried, or rather is inherited and re-enacted by current policy, practice, debates and problems.

Keywords Planning history · Liquor licensing · Local option · Temperance · Domestic violence · Australia

By 1922 when the *Old England Hotel* closed via the 1920 local option poll, my maternal grandmother was 6 years old and living amidst a local social norm of teetotalism with which she stuck for life, the occasional rumoured shandy excepted. While in taped interviews she recalls the doddering presence of her once violently drunken grandfather Jack Wilkinson, she also remembers (with mild irritation) the late nights of sober singing

© The Author(s) 2019

E. J. Taylor, *Dry Zones*, https://doi.org/10.1007/978-981-13-2787-2_6

of her parents and their Methodist friends. In my lifetime, the former *Old England Hotel* has been a quiet antiques store then a home, a slightly eccentric relic of the past. What was once the *Live and Let Live* hotel run by my paternal grandmother's family was marked only with a memorial stone, and I did not know of its existence, nor its family connection, until researching this story and with the help of my Aunt Pamela.

There are longer echoes of the Jack Wilkinson of the start of this book, and of people like him, their families, and of the temperance movement that took form around them over generations. In his family some of these attitudes and practices have been passed on to me albeit in much faded form. I have, as often as not, had a glass of wine beside me when writing this book. Yet Methodism—certain attitudes to work, and to signs of weakness—are harder norms to shake. In the wake of John Wilkinson's 1882 stint in prison, the rest of the Wilkinsons had joined the anti-alcohol Independent Order of Rechabites. Their involvement with the Rechabites could have been because of their own experiences, or because of the extent of Rechabite and Methodist temperance activity in the district. It is hard not to imagine that being active in one or more temperance organisations was part and parcel of social life and norms in the area.

The Normington and Lupton sides of my family (my father's mother) were also enmeshed in the Rechabites and temperance of the Victorian goldfields, but without as evangelical an origin story The Luptons and Normingtons appear to have ranged across running the *Live and Let Live Hotel*, to joining the Rechabites and local churches, to working in local temperance hotels, to comically lapsed efforts at non-drinking. Local news reports show them being periodically ejected from temperance institutions for drunkenness. The Harcourt and Barkers Creek district also featured in the start of A.B. Facey's canonical autobiography *A Fortunate Life*—a lifetime non-drinker, Facey had sworn to his grandmother, a Carr, to never drink alcohol. Facey's family, like mine, had been active in the Harcourt and Barkers Creek Rechabites (e.g. "Harcourt", *Mount Alexander Mail*, March 5, 1897, p. 2), and being temperate defined many of Facey's experiences and perspectives after leaving the district. Facey shared in the district's strong belief in improving life through sobriety. Even so, Facey in *A Fortunate Life* summarises his chapter on Barkers Creek with the austere quote "many people had little feeling or sympathy for those in need" (Facey 1985).

In the past few decades Harcourt and Barkers Creek have acquired several liquor licenses: 3 boutique cider producers and 5 wineries—all catering to the gentrified social-drinking population of Castlemaine, and facilitated by the liquor licensing and tax system categories which, particularly in recent decades, have supported the resurgence of Australian wine and cider industries. Harcourt has one "general" or hotel type license: a converted motel catering to recreational bicycle riders. Incongruous though this may seem to temperance adherents—some of who were known at one stage to also find bicycles morally offensive, at least on Sundays—the model of pub that the temperance movement fought and created (the "swill" pub, Dunstan's "late Edwardian urinal")—is a declining land use in Victoria generally, and an extinct one in Harcourt's surrounds. This is the same region that fought off en masse through the courts one of the newer forms of vice, gaming machines. It is the same region that can become as divided over a supermarket, a chicken farm (Butt and Taylor 2018), or a fast food restaurant as it once was over pubs in the local option era. Wowsers are dead–long live the wowsers.

More so than the old hotels of Harcourt and Barkers Creek, I used to have a stronger sense of the past of that place from a nearby bridge, on the side of the road near over the railway bridge to Specimen Gulley Road. The idea that pubs could ever have existed down that road into the sleepy bushland, which the Specimen Gully Quarry (or Platt's) Hotel did for some decades, remains extraordinary to me. On the stone bridge was painted a large and slowly-fading graffiti message declaring "HAPPY NYE, 1984". As each year passed the message on the bridge seemed the more out of place—stuck, somehow, still wearing the exuberance of those facing an unfolding future. It seemed ever more incongruous as the message faded into the landscape. The bridge, like the Old England hotel, is protected through a planning heritage overlay. Situated in a Rural Living Zone, the scene is unlikely to outwardly change, frozen into a kind of pastiche of early twentieth century rural Australia (cars and freeways excepted).

At least one history of the Australian goldfields era analogised the past as a hole from which stories can sometimes be unearthed, with effort, in garbled form (e.g. Wickham 2007). Something—instinct, Adam Smith's invisible hand of the market, Gatsby's green light—drives attention forward to the future as if it were completely novel, even when it is sometimes just as much a drive into a repeating past. In this book

I have sought to question whether history in liquor licensing and planning is simply buried, or is so intrinsic to current practice that we are effectively still re-enacting it. Certainly forgetfulness is a theme recognised by other work on liquor licensing: as in "it is striking, although not surprising, that many of the contemporary issues surrounding the role of alcohol in society preoccupied the attention of the intellectuals of previous generations" (McCoy 1988). Valverde (1998) concluded her book by recalling how: "the forgetful re-enactment of past debates is a major feature of contemporary debates on alcohol" (p. 203). Where violence is concerned, the past seems something we are particularly keen to keep forgetting.

Many decades after his stint in prison and local newspapers for attacking the publican of the Old England Hotel, formerly Walter's Hotel, the John "Jack" Wilkinson, one of my great-great-grandfathers, appeared, aged in his 80s, in more newspaper reports ("Castlemaine: Elderly Man Falls Down a Shaft", *Ballarat Star*, June 23, 1922; "Fell into Shaft: Elderly Man's Sufferings", *The Argus*, June 22, 1922). The 82 year old Wilkinson had been out on a walk in the old gold diggings around Castlemaine and fallen into a disused mine shaft 10 metres deep. This was the same year, of course, that the Old England was de-licensed by local option vote, marking the demise of the last of the area's hotels.

My grandmother recalled that in his old age her grandfather lived in the Castlemaine Benevolent Home, paid for by his children but not living with them, as (in another oblique reference to domestic violence) "his family didn't want him because he'd been such a rotten old thing". Often on his walks he visited her in Harcourt, dubbing her "little Jacko" (would that make me a "little little little Jacko?"). On this day he failed to return from his walk, and a search party was raised. Wilkinson remained trapped in the mine shaft for days, before being heard by a passer-by on a bicycle. My grandmother recalls how despite his advanced age, Wilkinson "was as strong as a bullock"—inadvertently using the same colonial term, "bullock" as in the description of his assault of Walter the publican in 1882. He had spent the time in the shaft trying to escape, repeatedly scaling up the sides before falling down again. He was hauled out with ropes by a rescue party, at which point, as my grandmother recalls:

> All he said was he swore at them and said '*why didn't you find me earlier!?*'. That made newspaper headlines in those days. That's how tough he was.

Jack Wilkinson had been trapped, by my grandmother's memory, for three days but by the newspaper reports a bit over one day. In any case when he was rescued, in this foul mood, swearing (as always), all the fingernails on his hands had been torn off from his efforts to escape the hole.

References

Butt, A., & Taylor, E. (2018). Smells like politics: Planning and the inconvenient politics of intensive peri-urban agriculture. *Geographical Research, 56*(2), 206–218.

Facey, A. B. (1985). *A fortunate life*. Ringwood: Penguin.

McCoy, D. A. (1988). Issues for Irish alcohol policy: A historical perspective with some lessons for the future. *Journal of the Statistical and Social Inquiry Society of Ireland, 26*, 1.

Valverde, M. (1998). *Diseases of the will: Alcohol and the dilemmas of freedom*. Cambridge and New York: Cambridge University Press.

Wickham, D. (2007). Silent screams: The hidden agenda. In K. Reeves & D. Nichols (Eds.), *Deeper leads: New approaches to Victorian goldfields history*. Ballarat: Ballarat Heritage Services.

Newspaper Articles

"Castlemaine: Elderly man falls down a shaft", *Ballarat Star*, June 23, 1922.

"Fell into shaft: Elderly man's sufferings", *The Argus*, June 22, 1922.

CHAPTER 7

Appendices

Abstract In the appendices to "Dry Zones", some of the key legislative changes to liquor licensing and planning in Victoria referred to within the book are listed or summarized in table form. The appendices tabulate known results (and legal challenges) to local option polls on licensing in Victoria over 1886–1906; the results of the 1920 local option poll by licensing districts; corresponding 1921 Census characteristics; a timeline of residential amenity and zoning controls on licensed premises in Victoria for indicative years (1850s to 2018); and a timeline of objection rights and neighbourhood rights against licensed premises in Victoria for indicative years (1850s to 2018).

Keywords Planning history · Liquor licensing · Property rights
Zoning · Local option

7.1 Appendix: Local Option Poll Results 1886–1906

The first local option poll under the 1885 system, Sale in 1886, was successful in voting for license reduction—but met with legal challenges over the amount of compensation. Although the Act specifically precluded depriving of a license without compensation, at that stage sufficient compensation funds had not been gathered.

Several polls in 1888 were successful but met with lengthy legal challenges—Geelong North, Port Melbourne, and South Williamstown

© The Author(s) 2019

E. J. Taylor, *Dry Zones*, https://doi.org/10.1007/978-981-13-2787-2_7

among them. The Port Melbourne and South Williamstown polls seem to have been disputed in court for so long that the Licensing Court was held to no longer have jurisdiction, and thus the reductions were never enforced. Port Melbourne met a similar fate—with sufficient votes for license reduction, but inertia in the process of delicensing.

In what seems to be the first case of license reductions actually enforced, the town of Rochester in Victoria's north held a successful poll in 1888 voting to reduce hotel numbers from 10 to 4. Although there were court disputes over which hotels to delicense, the process seems to have been implemented (Table 7.1).

Table 7.1 Known results (and legal challenges) to local option polls on licensing, 1886–1906

Year	*Location*	*Poll type and result*
1886	Sale	Successful vote to decrease hotel numbers Legal issues—objections around compensation
1886	Bacchus Marsh	To increase: 57 to increase, 26 against
1886	Bright	Insufficient votes
1886	Kyneton	Insufficient votes
1886	Maryborough	Insufficient votes
1886	Rosedale	Insufficient votes
1887	Benalla	Insufficient votes
1887	Warrnambool	Insufficient votes
1888	Castlemaine	Unsuccessful: 288 for existing (51 hotels), 145 for reduction (to 12 hotels)
1888	Geelong North	Successful poll to close 18 hotels, following Supreme Court case June 1888
1888	Port Melbourne	Successful poll to reduce (March 1888). Stand off re: number of votes. Another successful poll (substantial majority for reduction). However, mired in legal disputes: seemingly never enforced
1888	South Williamstown	Successful poll to reduce (March 1888) Supreme Court Cases in November 1888 and July 1889—seeking to stop the licensing court from determining which hotels to be closed, and questioning the validity of the poll (the inspector had died). Supreme Court upheld the poll. "Lengthy argument" about validity of polls, calculation of the statutory number. By the time the legal disputes were settled the Licensing Court no longer had jurisdiction to close the hotels

Table 7.1 (continued)

Year	*Location*	*Poll type and result*
1888	Warrnambool	Failed: reduction 346, continuance 394
1888	Ballarat East	Successful: 1242 for reduction, 423 for continuance. However a legal challenge over validity of the poll process
1888	Rochester	Successful vote to decrease from 10 to 4 hotels. 1888 Court case to decide which hotels to close
1890	Northcote	Insufficient votes
1890	Williamstown	Successful poll to reduce. Never enforced (legal issues)
1892	Eaglehawk	Failed by 90 votes
1900	Arcadia	To increase: Insufficient votes
1901	Broadford	To increase: Insufficient votes
1902	North Melbourne	Successful vote to reduce numbers by 37 (from 57 to 20). Arbitration courts 1904. 37 hotels finally closed in 1905
1903	Arcadia	To increase: Insufficient votes
1905	Barrabool	To increase: successful. 430 for, 43 against

7.2 Appendix: State-Wide Local Poll Results 1920

See Tables 7.2 and 7.3.

Table 7.2 Result of the local option poll—from Victoria Government Gazette No. 207, Friday November 19, 1920

Licensing district	*No on roll*	*Continuance*	*Reduction*	*No-license*	*Informal*	*Total votes polled*
Collingwood East	6315	2362	138	876	37	3413
North Richmond	9093	3406	159	1203	57	4825
Beaconsfield	8570	3279	482	1356	173	5290
Canterbury	12,981	4446	587	2738	210	7981
Clunes	1508	475	79	486	7	1047
Creswick	1637	538	46	447	16	1047
Dowling Forest	1853	627	43	304	14	988
Lexton	424	160	3	43	3	209
Ballaarat East	10,034	3340	283	3525	266	7414
Ballaarat West	10,477	3576	531	3652	188	7947
Barrabool	2536	679	138	803	39	1659
Lara	2040	736	108	520	42	1406
Newton and Chilwell	3963	1199	241	1360	90	2890
Queenscliff	3275	1204	203	738	70	2215
Benalla	3176	1010	125	568	40	1743
Mokoan	1786	482	100	416	30	1028
Yarrawonga	2889	1146	118	565	43	1872
Towong	3210	930	113	658	44	1745
Wodonga	1505	589	168	80	31	868
Yackandandah	1897	648	73	322	47	1090
Barkly (Bendigo)	4755	1880	176	1286	110	3452
Darling (Bendigo)	2654	1063	89	626	63	1841
Strathfieldsaye	928	393	41	150	20	604
Golden Square	6664	2294	259	2168	143	4864
Kangaroo Flat	2500	783	96	684	79	1642
Boroondara	14,358	2626	783	5845	208	9462
Caulfield East	14,355	2981	548	4049	158	7736

(continued)

Table 7.2 (continued)

Licensing district	*No on roll*	*Continuance*	*Reduction*	*No-license*	*Informal*	*Total votes polled*
Malvern East	13,426	2715	583	4527	156	7981
Nunawading	4298	820	177	1844	57	2898
Oakleigh	2086	543	65	612	35	1255
Birchip	1848	604	70	527	46	1247
Dunmunkle	2334	855	78	634	40	1607
Warracknabeal	3525	1081	176	1220	84	2561
Brighton	7941	1968	451	2295	84	4798
Elsternwick	6659	1294	232	1520	66	3112
Moorabbin	11,369	2460	434	3262	147	6303
Brunswick	25,240	8270	898	6048	343	15,559
Bacchus Marsh	1773	666	94	435	30	1225
Broadmeadows	2541	708	76	497	27	1308
Gisborne	1871	681	89	359	25	1154
Melton	3053	983	145	567	36	1731
Wyndham	2122	654	90	438	23	1205
Cardigan	6826	2582	113	710	48	3453
Princes Hill	6617	2879	93	787	47	3806
Castlemaine	3373	1289	173	1026	62	2550
Fryers	731	293	29	192	18	532
Maldon	1326	334	61	502	21	918
Taradale	1174	367	48	399	12	826
Barkly (Collingwood)	3730	1714	117	694	76	2601
Clifton Hill (Collingwood)	6598	2619	293	1523	103	4538
Darling	5061	2186	245	987	69	3487
Kilmore	1757	740	90	425	45	1300
Kyneton	3328	1517	169	933	69	2688
Lancefield	1485	571	100	444	37	1152

(continued)

Table 7.2 (continued)

Licensing district	*No on roll*	*Continuance*	*Reduction*	*No-license*	*Informal*	*Total votes polled*
Pyalong	481	247	21	84	10	362
Berwick	4458	1271	206	1011	76	2564
Dandenong	6261	1613	230	1575	125	3543
Mulgrave	4304	886	121	1228	49	2284
Scoresby	2541	584	102	751	28	1465
Bullarook	588	152	25	107	12	296
Daylesford	1666	632	71	387	23	1113
Franklin	1667	635	63	358	27	1083
Newstead	813	297	33	215	4	549
Trentham	1637	595	93	262	16	966
Arapiles	1381	317	53	422	26	818
Balmoral	633	257	34	138	17	446
Edenhope	1951	656	138	465	56	1315
Hamilton	4285	1539	155	1415	113	3222
Bridgewater	1482	584	79	386	43	1092
Eaglehawk	2759	982	111	1026	75	2194
Huntly	1713	671	73	473	52	1269
Runnymede	602	281	25	141	19	466
Gipps	2410	919	86	376	46	1427
Jolimont	7920	2627	397	1184	141	4349
Latrobe	1695	543	80	207	26	856
Ascotvale	6793	2004	305	1560	56	3925
Coburg	9336	2578	397	2771	138	5884
Essendon	4910	1328	337	1682	46	3393
Moonee Ponds	10,305	3216	523	2998	123	6860
Eltham	2380	666	133	526	55	1380
Healesville	1187	440	31	263	17	751

(continued)

Table 7.2 (continued)

Licensing district	*No on roll*	*Continuance*	*Reduction*	*No-license*	*Informal*	*Total votes polled*
Lilydale	6167	1760	333	2066	126	4285
Whittlesea	2218	585	129	629	37	1380
Central Fitzroy	4495	1809	151	637	63	2660
Clifton	4131	1437	143	962	53	2595
South Fitzroy	6141	2404	185	714	84	3387
Flemington	9186	3460	165	1438	64	5127
Hotham	2826	1182	42	355	17	1596
North Footscray	10,862	3318	163	2340	74	5895
East Geelong	6365	2400	324	1755	135	4614
West Geelong	8170	2992	437	2403	162	5994
Dargo	1103	349	48	340	49	786
Omeo	1327	626	54	281	25	986
Orbost	2431	675	85	571	57	1388
Tambo	1274	371	64	374	19	828
Avon	1320	433	82	365	34	914
Bairnsdale	2998	1055	133	827	66	2081
Maffra	2798	948	136	698	68	1850
Sale	2024	764	96	658	49	1567
Alberton	2970	774	163	683	62	1682
Rosedale	1183	347	79	246	15	687
Traralgon	3364	833	147	992	62	2034
Welshpool	2178	627	124	542	55	1348
Drouin	3079	684	80	583	25	1372
Mirboo	1506	357	51	370	9	787
Warragul	2633	482	86	799	23	1390
Woorayl	2353	546	55	596	42	1239
Banxholme	2350	696	89	837	118	1740

(continued)

Table 7.2 (continued)

Licensing district	*No on roll*	*Continuance*	*Reduction*	*No-license*	*Informal*	*Total votes polled*
Casteron	3337	1170	120	917	160	2367
Heywood	1481	361	50	607	63	1081
Portland	1863	676	108	578	76	1438
Arcadia	1162	391	62	275	19	747
Katamatite	1045	415	27	243	14	699
Numurkah	3216	959	156	1045	70	2230
Shepparton	3243	1037	121	1123	39	2320
Buninyong	1994	823	55	631	60	1569
Pitfield	1185	482	50	336	40	908
Sebastopol	1751	626	51	628	47	1352
Boort	974	283	41	333	11	668
Kerang	5548	1718	292	1988	166	4164
Terrick	1053	286	31	357	22	696
Wycheproof	1403	486	62	437	22	1007
Beaufort	2438	661	89	569	69	1388
Camperdown	5731	1809	248	1433	118	3608
Mortlake	1751	462	85	424	40	1011
Wickliffe	1438	398	63	418	37	916
Hawthorn	19,141	5071	1200	5694	224	12,189
Kew	9799	2196	589	3198	100	6083
Heidelberg	8088	2055	378	2797	107	5337
Northcote	17,648	5188	730	5180	220	11,318
North Fitzroy	3891	1334	164	970	29	2497
Preston	4928	1439	210	1270	37	2956
Dunolly	1955	830	107	556	62	1555
Landsborough	981	434	32	236	30	732
St Arnaud	1585	812	42	351	25	1230

(continued)

Table 7.2 (continued)

Licensing district	*No on roll*	*Continuance*	*Reduction*	*No-license*	*Informal*	*Total votes polled*
Stuart Mill	1827	731	71	610	52	1464
Charlton	2483	967	68	589	34	1658
Inglewood	1584	556	77	264	29	926
Serpentine	1010	263	41	243	30	577
Wedderburn	1767	528	90	535	46	1199
Dimboola	3091	1197	110	744	52	2103
Horsham	3327	976	167	1074	54	2271
Lawloit	1174	390	29	337	23	779
Nhill	1979	716	69	499	32	1316
Carisbrook	489	211	15	140	19	385
Maryborough	2797	1219	59	863	101	2242
Talbot	2232	786	64	559	56	1465
Timor	1387	513	39	355	38	945
Bourke	7661	3371	235	750	111	4467
Lonsdale	1191	426	54	145	9	634
Flinders	1836	647	72	423	32	1174
Jeetho	3640	931	163	989	44	2127
Mornington	3228	1000	153	727	59	1939
Phillip Island	7094	1930	218	1476	82	3706
North Carlton	7172	2493	215	1692	94	4494
North Melbourne	7969	3736	186	1042	115	5079
Royal Park	2411	725	70	639	17	1451
Beechworth	2341	971	47	422	26	1466
Bright	2148	740	39	422	18	1219
Chiltern	806	374	15	50	5	444
Corangamite	6179	2003	348	2074	190	4615
Leigh	1242	500	37	292	25	854

(continued)

Table 7.2 (continued)

Licensing district	*No on roll*	*Continuance*	*Reduction*	*No-license*	*Informal*	*Total votes polled*
Otway	1555	467	62	417	32	978
Winchelsea	2007	653	112	595	44	1404
Koroit	2733	1039	46	475	28	1588
Minhamite	940	283	13	224	8	528
Penshurst	1558	402	30	363	22	817
Port Fairy	2797	1118	38	261	17	1434
Emerald Hill	8149	3815	275	1014	143	5247
Port Melbourne	7880	3562	331	1240	169	5302
Prahran	9145	3130	483	1827	150	5590
South Yarra	11,533	3531	888	2362	144	6925
Central Richmond	10,914	3843	235	1587	51	5716
South Richmond	6469	2331	177	1077	57	3642
Echuca	2356	821	75	438	59	1393
Mooroopna	3869	1080	171	1147	76	2474
Rochester	3231	1000	137	911	80	2128
Rochester East	1874	651	73	545	37	1306
Ararat	2113	857	107	496	39	1499
Glenorchy	1727	595	72	364	40	1071
Moyston	1747	614	94	364	28	1100
Stawell	2456	1075	76	516	77	1744
Balaclava	10,019	2962	581	2061	118	5722
Caulfield	10,791	2301	567	3017	103	5988
St Kilda East	6067	1779	392	1088	80	3339
St Kilda West	7258	2059	484	1057	68	3668
Corong	5047	1534	118	982	111	2745
Mildura	6530	1419	68	928	89	2504
Swan Hill	6042	1957	146	1496	128	3727
Armadale	10,803	2694	691	2525	178	6088

(continued)

Table 7.2 (continued)

Licensing district	*No on roll*	*Continuance*	*Reduction*	*No-license*	*Informal*	*Total votes polled*
Malvern	7305	1848	457	2203	102	4610
Toorak	6617	1587	544	1474	75	3680
Alexandra	2162	724	161	387	45	1317
Mansfield	1769	713	68	359	40	1180
Seymour	1718	553	102	358	52	1065
Strathbogie	1094	331	60	352	37	780
Yea	1424	449	49	273	29	800
Narracan	2574	708	80	665	55	1508
Walhalla	1242	390	54	249	26	719
Wood's Point	2597	719	62	455	40	1276
Oxley	1903	544	27	278	24	873
Peechelba	No poll held					
Rutherglen	2138	1240	48	141	21	1450
Wangaratta	3074	1220	52	511	22	1805
Goulburn	2702	1053	95	683	59	1890
Heathcote	2036	780	89	410	40	1319
Rushworth	2322	970	156	498	69	1693
Ballan	1888	737	45	209	15	1006
Bungaree	1931	649	22	319	20	1010
Meredith	673	251	8	112	7	378
Warrenheip	1128	480	9	116	11	616
Allansford	2642	824	101	861	72	1858
Cobden	2270	689	91	603	52	1435
Warrnambool	4426	1624	218	1496	86	3424
Footscray	11,389	4021	204	2470	63	6758
North Williamstown	6485	2129	158	1700	31	4018
South Williamstown	5407	1921	124	1199	33	3277

Table 7.3 1921 census and 1920 local option poll votes, by licensing districts (averages)

	No license	*Reduction*	*Continuance*	*All districts*
Number of districts	2	71	144	218
Size of district (electoral roll)	9328	4687	3614	4020
Roman Catholic (% of district population)	8.8	17.6	23.8	21.7
Methodist (% of district population)	16.7	14.8	11.8	12.8
Female (% of district population)	52.9	49.9	49.3	49.6
Voter turnout (%)	66.7	65.0	62.45	63.3
No license (% of vote)	64.0	48.2	33.6	38.7
Reduction (% of vote)	7.3	7.4	6.1	6.5
Continuance (% of vote)	28.6	44.4	59.6	54.4
No license and reduction (combined %)	71.4	55.6	39.7	45.2

7.3 Appendix: Timeline of Amenity and Objection Rights Around Liquor Licensing in Victoria

See Tables 7.4 and 7.5.

Table 7.4 Timeline of residential amenity and zoning controls on licensed premises, Victoria (indicative years)

Licensing Act year	*Amenity-related grounds for objection—liquor licenses*	*Zoning separation*
1864	Near a church, hospital or school; will disturb quiet	–
1885	Not required; near a church, hospital, or school; will disturb quiet	Residential covenants become more common in subdivisions: protecting low density brick houses from other uses including hotels Public health and nuisance by-laws more common
1915	Not required; near a church, hospital, or school; will disturb quiet	Residential covenants. Public health and building regulations. Local Government Act—by-laws expand: residential zones, (anti) flat codes. Some municipalities apply local residential zoning
1954	Not required; near a church, hospital, or school; will disturb quiet	State level legislation for town planning introduced 1944. Combined with local zoning–for example Box Hill residential zone by-law ("council-prescribed residential area") First implemented metropolitan level plan, Melbourne Metropolitan Planning Scheme, introduced 1954 Residential zones under MMBW zoning excluded hotels from Residential "A", "B". Like funeral parlours, hotels had existing use rights to stay but were essentially prohibited in residential areas moving forward Minimum off-street parking requirements applied to any new hotels in other areas. (1 per 20 feet of public bar, 1 per 60 feet of hotel lounge or beer garden)
1968	Not required; near a church, hospital, or school; will disturb quiet (for hotels only)	Zoning and planning controls Environmental Protection Act 1970: implications for noise, septic tanks

(continued)

Table 7.4 (continued)

Licensing Act year	*Amenity-related grounds for objection—liquor licenses*	*Zoning separation*
1987	Impact on the *amenity* of the locality: a license or licensing change would "detract from or be detrimental to the amenity of the area"	Zoning including residential zones that exclude uses other than homes, places of worship, schools Minimum car parking requirements—Victoria Planning Provisions 52.06 minimum car parking requirements 52.27 Licensed premises—require planning permit in any area
1998 (current in 2018)	Impact on the *amenity* of the locality: under the *Liquor Control Reform Act 1998* amenity is defined as "the quality of an area that is pleasant and agreeable". Including car parking facilities, traffic, noise, "the possibility of nuisance or vandalism", and "the harmony and coherence of the environment"	Zoning including Reformed Residential Zones. As of right uses: low-density dwellings, place of worship (church), school. Food and drink premises except convenience restaurant stores (on main roads) prohibited uses 52.06 minimum car parking requirements for hotels or taverns–0.4 spaces per patron, or 3.5 spaces per 100 sqm (new premises) 52.27 Licensed premises–require permit in any area. Also to extend hours, etc. "To ensure that the impact of the licensed premises on the amenity of the surrounding area is considered" Environmental protection–noise guidelines. State Environment Protection Policy (Control of Music Noise from Public Premises) Criminal and public by-laws on drinking and drunkenness in public spaces–combined police and local government "dry areas"

(continued)

Table 7.5 Timeline of objection rights/neighbourhood rights against licensed premises, Victoria (indicative years)

Year	*Vetting powers: Number of licenses in area*	*Vetting powers: Individual license applications*
1853	–	If a "memorial in writing signed by five persons residing in the immediate vicinity" said the licensee had infringed conditions, then justices could refuse license
1864	–	Objections could be heard against applications including if "in the immediate vicinity of a place of public worship hospital or school". Also "if the quiet of the place…will be disturbed"—and if a petition were signed by "a majority of the occupiers of houses in the immediate neighbourhood"
1870	Municipal bodies could object to a license in a district if there were already sufficient number of licensed premises–if so, license applications were to be refused	Ratepayers in district could object to application or renewal including if "in the immediate vicinity of a place of public worship hospital or school". Also if the license "is not required in the neighbourhood"
1876	All new license numbers in districts frozen "until the ratepayers of such municipal district" vote to allow an increase to a given number All districts (based on municipalities) to have vote every 3 years to decide whether to increase. If a majority vote for no increase, then no new licenses	Objections could be heard "if the quiet of the place…will be disturbed"—or "not required" in area, near place of worship hospital or school. If a petition were signed by "a majority of the ratepayers in at the neighbourhood object"—then the magistrates had to refuse license. "Neighbourhood" as defined by the magistrates
1885	Voluntary petitions by rate paying electors could ask to hold a ballot and determine whether to decrease licenses to the "statutory number"—roughly 1 hotel per 250 population Districts could also petition and vote for whether to increase to the statutory number. No new licenses allowed above the statutory number Licensing Courts enforced local option decision if vote for reduction. The licensing courts determined which to deprive	Objections could be heard "if the quiet of the place…will be disturbed"—or "not required" in area, near place of worship hospital or school. If a petition were signed by "a majority of the ratepayers in at the neighbourhood object"—then the magistrates had to refuse license Exceptions for hotels with 30 or more bedrooms: possible (though difficult) to gain license for very large premises

(continued)

Table 7.5 (continued)

Year	*Vetting powers: Number of licenses in area*	*Vetting powers: Individual license applications*
1906	Local electors could petition to increase to statutory number Statutory number License Reduction Board empowered to reduce licenses to statutory number (1 per 250 population). The licensing courts determined which to deprive	Objections allowed by "any ratepayer, freeholder or leaseholder of property situated within one mile from such premises"
1916	License Reduction Board empowered to reduce licenses by 25% in all areas. The Board determined which to deprive. All licenses by district frozen at existing number Mallee provisions: allowed new hotels by petition and vote in newly settled areas	
1920	Compulsory state-wide local option poll—licensing districts voted whether to continue, reduce license numbers by 25%, or "no license". 60% "no license" would deprive all license License Reduction Board enforced results of local option polls by determining which to deprive, and what compensation to pay	
1922	Local option polls: could only vote for "no license" or continuance. Polls only every 8 years. LRB could reduce by 25% in any district	
1928	Local option polls: could only vote for "no license" or continuance. Polls only every 8 years. LRB could reduce by 25% in any district	Objections could be heard "if the quiet of the place…will be disturbed"—or "not required" in area, near place of worship hospital or school If a petition from ratepayers of any local government area (subject to proof of authenticity) appears that a majority of the ratepayers in the neighbourhood object, the Licensing Court were to refuse the application

(continued)

Table 7.5 (continued)

Year	*Vetting powers: Number of licenses in area*	*Vetting powers: Individual license applications*
1953	Local option deleted from licensing Act in 1946	Dry areas: court orders that in the 2 dry zones, electors' polls would be held on every license application. Neighbourhood means the surroundings, delineated by the Court and Chief Electoral Officer. Local option polls of electors (Licensing Act 1958). If refused, not to grant nor for 3 years afterwards
1965	LRB assessment of need for premises	Dry areas: dry zone/electors' polls on all license applications Other areas: if 3 or more petitioned with 50+ signatures, the LRB defined an area. If after a month it appeared the majority opposed the license, it was refused. Objectors had to be resident in the relevant subdivision
1968	Major changes to licensing categories and approaches Assessment of new licenses still included "the licensed premises re not required in the neighbourhood"	Dry areas: dry zone/electors' polls on all license applications Other areas: if 3 or more petitioned with 50+ signatures, the LRB defined an area. If after a month it appeared the majority of electors opposed the license, it was refused. Objectors had to be resident in the relevant subdivision Third-party objections on planning permit decisions
1987	Recommendation on community interest	Liberalisation: Third-party objection rights in *Planning and Environment Act*. Merit-based Also community or police objections under *Licensing Reform Act* 1987. Grounds of amenity. No petition system In dry areas: dry zone/electors' polls on all license applications Third party objections on planning permit decisions

(continued)

Table 7.5 (continued)

Year	*Vetting powers: Number of licenses in area*	*Vetting powers: Individual license applications*
1998 (Current 2018)	From 2007: Designated Areas declared by police and licensing commission. 20 areas subject to additional controls From 2011: Freeze on late night licenses in inner city municipalities From 2015: Cumulative Impact on amenity, whether there is insufficient need. For packaged alcohol–alcohol-related harm Municipalities and police consulted on applications–recommendation on community interest Gaming machine applications–cap on total numbers, and from 2006 per-capita caps by region	*Recognising Objectors Bill* 2015–"The responsible planning authority must (where appropriate) have regard to the number of objectors in considering whether the use or development may have a significant social effect." Also community or police objections under Licensing Reform Act. Grounds of amenity and social impact, insufficient need In dry areas: dry zone/electors' polls on license applications excluding café and applications Gaming machine applications (must be in licensed premises)—number of objections is part of social benefit/disbenefit assessment

The manufacturer's authorised representative in the EU is Springer Nature Customer Service Centre GmbH, Europaplatz 3, 69115 Heidelberg, Germany. If you have any concerns regarding our products, please contact ProductSafety@springernature.com

Printed and bound by CPI Group (UK) Ltd, Croydon, CR0 4YY
25/09/2026
02222902-0015